COLLISION OF WORLDS

COLLISION OF WORLDS

◆

A Priest's Life

Charles R. Colwell

6/24/08

*To Thomas & Susan —
You are two very special persons.
I'm so grateful our lives have crossed
& hope it continues.
God bless you all.
With great affection.
Charles R. Colwell*

iUniverse, Inc.
New York Bloomington Shanghai

COLLISION OF WORLDS
A Priest's Life

Copyright © 2008 by Charles R. Colwell

All rights reserved. No part of this book may be used or reproduced by any means, graphic, electronic, or mechanical, including photocopying, recording, taping or by any information storage retrieval system without the written permission of the publisher except in the case of brief quotations embodied in critical articles and reviews.

iUniverse books may be ordered through booksellers or by contacting:

iUniverse
1663 Liberty Drive
Bloomington, IN 47403
www.iuniverse.com
1-800-Authors (1-800-288-4677)

Because of the dynamic nature of the Internet, any Web addresses or links contained in this book may have changed since publication and may no longer be valid.

The views expressed in this work are solely those of the author and do not necessarily reflect the views of the publisher, and the publisher hereby disclaims any responsibility for them.

ISBN: 978-0-595-48004-3 (pbk)
ISBN: 978-0-595-71507-7 (cloth)
ISBN: 978-0-595-60107-3 (ebk)

Printed in the United States of America

For my beloved wife Judy,
my last blind date,
who has shown me the face of Love,
with profound thanks
and pigeon feathers.

Contents

Foreword... xi
Preface xiii
CHAPTER 1   No Balm in Gilead: Doubt 1
CHAPTER 2   Encountering Dragons........................... 14
CHAPTER 3   Demythologizing the Priesthood 33
CHAPTER 4   Embracing the Secular.......................... 52
CHAPTER 5   Radical Grace 61
CHAPTER 6   Neither Jew nor Greek: Interfaith Dialogue....... 70
CHAPTER 7   Shifting Sand around the Rock 89
Afterword 105
Notes 109

Acknowledgments

I want to acknowledge several people who have given many hours of their time and expertise in helping me make this project a reality.

One is Barbara Crafton, whose advice, support, and depth of life and ministry I greatly appreciate. She walked me through this process with clarity and gentle prodding and deftly critiqued the manuscript. I owe an enormous debt of gratitude to Sue Stanley, who labored for many months typing the various changes in the text. Her patience, humor, and generosity are outstanding. I am also grateful for the professional eye and suggestions of Caitlin Kelly, who is a wise and generous friend and author, and to Barry Seaman, retired editor for *Time* and author, for his generous comments, for his encouragement, and for his appetite for the subject of doubt. And, finally, I am grateful to the good people of the Church of St. Barnabas in Irvington, New York, who have provided me with grist for the mill for the exercise of ministry these past thirty-six years. We have walked many miles together, and God has, indeed, blessed our journey.

Foreword

We always meet at Charlie's church; six or eight of us have been coming there once a month for four years now. We used to spend the first hour in theological discussion of some topic that I would suggest, but something happened about a year into our history. Then we quit having a theme and just went around the circle, sharing the agony and the ecstasy and the tedium of ordained life. We didn't need a sacred topic; our very *lives* were sacred. We found God in them as we showed them to one another.

This book is just like that, a testament to the presence of the sacred in every square inch of what we so confidently call the secular. There *isn't* any sacred and secular, as far as Charlie is concerned; everything we behold is permeated with God. Those of us who can't see it should, perhaps, have our eyes checked. Or, better, find a companion or two to walk with along the way with us. We see a lot more when we walk together than when we go wandering off alone.

A life is lived in these chapters: almost half a century of ministry. A very human life, displayed with rueful honesty—Charlie is the oldest member of our group, but he is also the most irreverent. The wry twinkle in his eye becomes a flash of fire when he is indignant. He seems to have misplaced that manipulative sweetness one sometimes finds in religious people, although I suspect the truth is that he never had it in the first place. And all his sacred cows escaped a long time ago—Charlie, for instance, is famous among us for hating Christmas.

Much has happened during Charlie's long service in his lovely old church, a church that looks like it should be in a movie. Some of these events were profoundly moving. Some were funny. Some were frightening, and some were terribly sad. Reading this narrative is like sitting with Charlie in his office while we talk. The things he remembers remind you of what you remember. His struggles remind you of your own.

Barbara Cawthorne Crafton

Preface

In the forty-five years that I have served as a priest in Episcopal parishes in New York, I have repeatedly experienced the split between religious and secular, often expressed as opposites: religious versus secular, and spirit versus flesh. One of the most obvious incidents involved two men in the congregation. It was "Bring Up Sunday" in May, the weekend before our annual thrift sale. Hundreds of items, stored in the undercroft of the parish hall, needed to be taken upstairs and moved to a variety of departments for organization. Bart and Paul had discovered a large oil painting of a portly female nude and wanted to discard it. They showed it to women in charge of the sale, and the women asked, "What's wrong with selling it?" The women in turn, brought it to my office and asked me for advice.

"Why not sell it?" I responded. The nude painting was set up in the white elephant department; the next day it had vanished. There was no mystery as to who the culprits were! Bart and Paul felt it was their mission to keep the "secular" nude from contaminating the "religious" congregation. These two worlds were colliding.

The Latin word for secular, *saeculum*, is actually a neutral word meaning *worldly*, but it doesn't imply any of the negative meanings that have come to be associated with it. The church has tried to recover *secular* from the scrap heap by pointing out that both the Jews and the early Christians viewed the world as unified and felt that there is, in actuality, no division between religious and secular. Theologian J. A. T. Robinson shook the church on both sides of the Atlantic in the mid 1960s in his book, *Honest to God*, when he used phrases like "worldly believers" and "the holy in the common."[1] A rabbi friend of mine tells me that to Jews the word *secular* means ordinary, weekday, not special—to make a distinction from the Sabbath, which is special. In Christian history this split between body and spirit appears as early as the second century, when Gnosticism flourished, proclaiming a type of dualism. The Gnostics saw the world and all material things, including the human body, as evil. They didn't believe that God was the creator of flesh, but that a force of evil had created the material universe. Salvation meant freedom from the contamination of the world. They believed that God and these evil forces were in a constant battle for human souls. This view was rejected as heretical by orthodox Christianity because it held that Jesus was spirit and not flesh. Gnostics said that Jesus only appeared to be flesh and blood. They were sometimes called Docetists ("to seem"), believing that the Biblical view of Jesus as human as well as God was repugnant. The First Epistle of John was written to counter this view, and the Nicene Creed certainly corrects it, claiming a unity between flesh and spirit. Nevertheless, throughout the succeeding centuries, variations on the Gnostic distortion of the material world continued to reappear as the church struggled with a common split between *secular* and *religious,* much to the detriment of the Christian faith and the human psyche.

The centerpiece of Christianity is found in the Christmas story, i.e., in the Incarnation, the belief that God entered human flesh in Jesus and lived among us. This central tenet of Christianity holds together both flesh and spirit as parts of a whole. Spirit is anchored in flesh, and flesh is informed by spirit. In the Incarnation God declares *all* things holy. There is no such thing, for example, as *a Christian life.* There is only life. William Temple, the Archbishop of Canterbury in the 1930s, said that "Christianity is the most materialistic religion in the world," because God entered human flesh and declared it good.

I have discovered in my relationship with Judy, my wife of forty-four years, a laboratory in which I have found incarnate love at the center. Our marriage has helped me bring flesh and spirit together as one integrated whole. Judy is my greatest teacher and friend, showing me year by year what God and wholeness look like.

A collision of worlds is ever present in a priest's life. Many parishioners think that clergy never entertain doubt. Think again! Doubt and a variety of other dragons that need to be tamed become part of a priest's opportunity for growth.

Priesthood or ordained ministry is often viewed through the lens of numerous stereotypes held by clergy and laity alike. These myths need to be exposed so that the uniqueness of the priestly role can be uncovered. Part of the discovery is in breaking down the fictional wall that separates religious from secular. In the midst of this struggle, we find God's one-way love for us, which is called grace and which is unconditional and never-changing; this deeply affects the way we live and do ministry.

Living life as Christians is often myopic and self-centered, yet there are millions of others who are not Christian who are moving into our communities, marrying our children and requesting a place at the table. How do we see God at work in this new community? Is there room at the table for all of us? Bringing the religious and the secular together can help us understand St. Paul's phrase that "in Christ there is neither Jew nor Greek." (Romans 10:12)

Finally, I will suggest areas where the church needs to lighten up and shed some of its cherished fixed convictions; I will also suggest ways for the church to become more user-friendly to outsiders and more open to *new truths*, while remaining anchored to the Rock at the center of our faith.

The centerpiece, the unifying principle at the heart of ordained ministry, is the integration of religious and secular. It is my core conviction that we must not sell out to either, but must live in the creative tension between the two. Here lies the hope of salvation and peace. Promoting this integration is the *raison d'être* of serious ministry as well as life, energizing them and making them vital. I hope that you will join me in the pages of this book in embracing the secular as God's greatest sacrament and thus minimizing the collision of the worlds we navigate.

I have changed many names and details in order to honor rules of confidentiality.

Charles R. Colwell
Irvington-on-Hudson, New York
March, 2008

1

No Balm in Gilead: Doubt

○ ○
"Let darkness come upon you, which shall be the darkness of God."
—*T. S. Eliot*

Dark Night

After nineteen years as rector at St. Barnabas, I am finally going to take a six-month sabbatical. I am beginning this time with a long retreat sponsored by the Gilead Institute for Spiritual Formation. I have been drawn here by one of my favorite psychiatrist-authors, Dr. Henry Sites, who is on the staff. The retreat center is located in the rolling Pennsylvania hills about an hour west of Philadelphia. Last night, as forty of us gathered for the first time, the staff spoke personally and vulnerably of their own spiritual journeys. They are very real, open, and wise. The group is diverse and interesting. How blessed I am to be here in this safe, nurturing environment.

The next day I sit next to Henry Sites at lunch. What an exciting moment this is! As the conversation turns to the experience of grace, I share with him my discovery of radical grace, coming not from the Church or psychiatry but through the discovery of my addiction. There is no response. He turns to a woman across the table and works out a private appointment, gets up without a word, and leaves the table. I feel dismissed, insignificant, hurt, and angry. I guess I have looked to him as a father figure, mentor, and role model and have come seeking recognition and affirmation. Suddenly the safety of this place seems to be disappearing, and I feel like escaping and moving into busyness. I feel another agenda settling itself in me. I've come here to sit at this man's feet, and he is totally disinterested in me!

"What are you doing to me, God? How could I go from such comfort and safety to such dis-ease and fear in just a few hours? Please, Lord, speak to me and show me some kindness this afternoon, amidst my isolation, fear, and loneliness. Don't let this get too painful. We are about to enter five days of silent retreat. How can I survive? I get it, God—you have set me up to feel rejected, betrayed, and hurt so I can get to that place which is a seed of so much of my fear. It is lack of trust that is my issue. I really don't believe that I can trust you. Will you abandon me and leave me alone—unconnected, unnoticed, unrecognized?"

I begin the silent retreat, after an uneasy luncheon, with a walk to the river which turns into a metaphor for my life as an eight-year-old. I am surrounded by green, rolling fields and am flooded by the early smells of new-cut grass and clover. I have a vision of Riverside Cemetery in Hancock, Maine, where many of my relatives are buried. The sound of birds and crickets conspire with the smells to announce, "The grave is ready, and you are to remain here alone and forever. This is all there is." I hear a snake slither through the grass near my path. As an eight-year-old, I am scared of the walk, scared to be alone, scared of what might happen and of the unknown.

The path stretches out over one enormous hill to another. It is getting hot; I have to go the bathroom. I begin to climb the next hill as sweat pours from my brow. I am alone, really alone, and no one knows where I am. "Do you really care, God? I don't even trust that you are real. There, I said it and it feels honest. Screw you, God!" I find a hill off the beaten path, climb it, and urinate behind a scanty bush. Where is the river, for heaven's sake? There is no sign of it anywhere. The river is like God, a cruel illusion. "God, you have brought me out here to torture me and to let me die alone. You don't care about me. You are a huckster with evil intentions. Why do we call you Love?"

My father appears in my mind's eye. In fact he has recently moved from Maine to live with us after suffering from a mild stroke and dementia.

"Where are you, Dad? You never show up in the script! You were absent for most of my early years." (He was piloting lobster boats from Maine across the North Atlantic to Newfoundland.) "You never helped me with my fear. You never held me or hugged me. You were too busy, and you were a man, and men work too hard, which is supposed to be a virtue, and never say 'I love you,' or 'I am scared,' or 'I am proud of you.'" And the guilt grew, and I came to fear life. I feel scared, alone. "So, God, why are you not just like my father—removed and unknowable? You and I have walked many miles together, but on a deep level, I don't believe you are to be trusted. I believe you will leave me in the cemetery to bury myself. No one in attendance, just a quiet, tearless self-burial."

The beauty of this place just accents how alone I am. No one cares. I am truly abandoned. "I have prayed and pleaded, Lord, and all I get is your damned silence. Guess what? You are a sick joke. With friends like you, bring on the enemy! If I can't trust you, then nothing makes any sense. In fact, beauty isn't even beauty. It is a seductive, evil illusion. You and Henry Sites are in the same club."

The breeze is comforting, as are the last drops of sunlight. "The ball is in your court, God, but I'm scared to death that you won't come through for me." Butterflies begin appearing in my stomach as dusk approaches. This is a time when every absence becomes heightened. I dread facing another night alone and in silence. Oh, for Judy's arms! Hers is the only presence I really trust.

The evening session focuses on icons, a number of which are on easels around the meeting room. I feel drawn to the Russian icon of Our Lady of Vladimir. Even though I don't want to endorse Marianism, she mysteriously beckons me. I finally go upstairs to my room, exhausted but hungry for music. I put on my Walkman and listen to Mahler's "Resurrection Symphony #2":

> "What was created must perish,
> What has perished, rise again!
> Cease trembling!
> Prepare thyself to live!"

The next morning I am drawn to visit *my* icon again. My focus has become the point of contact—the baby Jesus pressed against Mary's cheek. This is the incarnational point where earth and heaven, flesh and spirit touch each other. I suddenly become the eight-year-old child on the cross. I am hanging there. I imagine Mary holding me as she does Jesus and feeling secure. I hear her say, "You are safe here, Charlie, truly safe. I'll take care of you. Nothing can touch you here. My love is the same love the Father has. You can bring all your fears here and be safe, Charlie. I love you."

By noon the doubts began to fill my mind once again. I'm going on a walk. "Will you go with me, Lord? You supposedly led me to the icon, but now you have ditched me. I feel like Estragon in *Waiting for Godot;* I hated that play, and I certainly hate this one." As the wind blows and the trees bend as if in mourning, I walk down the main road that leads to the retreat center. I begin an angry, passionate, and rage-filled conversation with the absent God. "You have let me down. You have put me through hell this week and uncovered a lot of buried conflict. I felt led to Our Lady of Vladimir—and for what? The retreat is over tomorrow, and I have no sign that I can trust you." I curse God for forty-five minutes. "Lord, I have just lost my faith in you! That means that my job as a priest goes with it, and much of the rest of my life. You bastard-trickster-God, you phony, non-existent thug! You are not even real! You don't exist!." Yes, I just said it, those awful words: *You don't exist.*

I am sitting in a late afternoon Silent Presence Group feeling exhausted and depleted—also disoriented and scared to death. "How can I live with my main point of reference removed? That deep, black-woods kind of fear. "Your move, O Absent One!" I want to run away, but I need to be with people. During the quiet time, I doze off and hear a woman's voice say: "Hang on, Charlie." The fight has gone out of me. I feel empty and as if I am on autopilot. I have little left to say or to do or to yell. I've put it all out there, and my tank is empty, and I'm coasting downhill for now. I feel that my anger toward God is very real, that it has integrity, and it feels authentic. "To the voice, whoever you are, I have nothing left to do but wait; I have little fight left."

We are gathered in the conference room for the late afternoon session. I refuse to look at "my icon." I'm not doing any more work. If I go home unrepaired, there is no way that I'm going to church on Sundays. That would be like being tossed into a caldron of boiling water. No more Daily Office, no more prayer; forget it all. I don't need it; it's useless anyway. Today is Ascension Day, The day Jesus ascended to heaven and promised the outpouring of the Spirit. Where is the Spirit? I share my story of what has been happening in our small group. I begin to cry when the others gather around me and lay their hands on my head and shoulders. I feel no resolution, but I do feel a bit of peace, a kind of detached serenity. Winnie suggests that I speak with Rose, a staff member, about what has been happening to me. I go for a walk with Rose and tell her the whole story. I like her; she is gentle, realistic, and wise. She recognizes that an incredible process has been going on this week and that she would be suspicious if it became resolved too quickly. She says, "God is stepping back just a bit so you can be free and allow time for things to happen. Charlie, don't work so hard; clarity will come. The God you've known needs to die so that the real one can take his place." Somehow her words are believable. I feel cleansed by the earlier explosion of rage against God. That, in a strange way, feels holy. So here I am with my issues all stirred up, going home unresolved, but at least they are on the table.

The sun sets, and the final session of the retreat begins. The Eucharist is a beautiful liturgy. We begin to sing, "God, Guide Me Home" and I begin to weep. I cannot believe what has happened! If I had known, I never would have come here. Surgery has been performed, but without closing the incision.

Waiting for Answers

It is wonderful to be able to share with Judy the whole nuanced story of what happened to me at Gilead. She is a gracious listener who truly understands. She doesn't try to fix me or give me too much advice. She is wise and gently present. She is struck by my feeling that God should have taken care of me on my own terms. She says, "You were trying to control God and tell him what to do and how to do it." She is also struck by my feeling that God had abused me. "Why blame him?" she asks. I go to bed around 1:45 AM and have a fitful sleep. Waking at four thirty, I hear my own voice say, "I am up against the searing heat of God's Love," At 7:00 AM, I hear God say, "I am willing to let you die that you may discover me."

I am still not ready to pray yet, but I have a strong impulse to do so; I don't want to force the issue. In three weeks I am scheduled to spend ten days at Holy Cross Monastery on the Hudson River, living the "Benedictine Experience," a balance of prayer, work, study, and rest. I want to cancel my reservation, but Judy insists that it is an essential piece of what is happening to me. At night, as I go to bed, Judy says to me, "Well, I guess your sabbatical has now started!"

I decide to go to an area church my first Sunday back but have very conflicted feelings, since I cannot bring myself to pray. I think I must stay here in this silent mode for a while. The music is painful, the words meaningless. Words, words, words. Empty, pious words! There is no good news here.

"We should do the most loving thing," the priest spits out. What does this mean? I hate this service and the sermon and this rote liturgy. I have a great desire to reach down into my life and to press the fast-forward button and to get past this most unpleasant part of my life's tape. I remember a passage by author John Gorsuch: "Who wants to swim far in the spiritual ocean if God turns out to be a shark?"[1]

A Letter to the God I Don't Believe in

Somehow, my most honest prayer is not to pray. It is tied to my integrity more than to stubbornness. "I do not want to short-circuit what I am feeling about you, God." For me, this is the deepest, most authentic prayer I can muster. I think back to Gilead and my battle with God on the windy road. It was a vicious, ultimate battle; my arrival at the point where I could reject God was somehow honest and pure. My rage was pure? How strange! I haven't prayed for many days. Many times each day, I begin and then stop suddenly when I sense the impulse. Although I feel uneasy, it seems right. I figure that if God cares, (and that is still on hold), that he will do whatever is necessary for my good even without my prayers. That really would be depending on grace. I know the advice to "fake it until you make it," but I'm not ready to do that with integrity yet. Can I trust God to take care of me and not abandon me? I must first deal with my feelings that he has injured and abused me. He's not off the hook yet! Somewhere deep in my heart or brain, a little piece of me knows that all will be well, that the power of self-will was broken on the retreat; that the God of *my* kingdom was defeated and that the independent and only God of the truly powerless was born. I do believe that this is a paradigm shift for me, but most of me is not there yet. I even regret articulating this, yet it feels right to let each voice within me have its say and forgo integration at the moment. It is largely out of my hands. "Well, God, I guess you mean business, but I also mean business. I do believe that the wrestling is important. I can't imagine just saying "yes" to you without engaging in a visceral fight with you. Jacob did the same in his dream. I feel little joy or beauty in my life even in this exploding time of spring, in music, or in relationships. My life is just a flat plain that goes on endlessly with little of interest or excitement. It's like the bottom has fallen out of my life. I feel myself disappearing."

Moving On

Looking through books on my library shelf, I find a quote from the second step in the *Alcoholics Anonymous* big book: "Came to believe that a Power greater than ourselves could restore us to sanity." Sounds good to me! Later, in talking to Douglas, my spiritual director, he says, "You have equated God with your own father, and you need to deal with that unfinished business." There does seem to be an opening in the darkness. Could it be that God has been moving through me, doing for me what I cannot accomplish on my own? "I remember St. Paul's words, "Likewise the Spirit helps us in our weakness; for we do not know how to pray as we ought, but the Spirit himself intercedes for us with sighs too deep for words." (Romans 8:26) Can I trust this process without controlling it? I am suspending all judgment in order to allow God to reshape whatever it is he wants. This passive position isn't my most comfortable place. Damn! It all seems so elusive. Is it, perhaps, all a dream? I feel that I am not meant to attempt any conscious resolution with God; I must trust the process. The response comes as I lay in bed one night: "*All* will be well—let *me* do it, Charlie. You are going to be safe. This is *my* work." These are uncharted waters for me, going against everything in my nature. "*I'm* doing the work this time, Charlie." Wow! This is a new ball game. What are the rules? What inning are we in? What's the score? Who's up at bat?

I open the Office Book to the Psalms for the fourteenth morning. I stare at the words of Psalm 71, which begins, "In you, O Lord, have I taken refuge …" Am I meant to begin praying again? Is it too soon? Oh hell, here goes. "In you, O Lord, have I taken refuge … be my strong rock, a castle to keep me safe; you're my crag and my stronghold. O God, be not far from me. I shall always wait in patience and shall praise you more and more. You have showed me great troubles and adversities, but you will restore my life and bring me up again from the deep places of the earth."

I step out of the supermarket and reach for my car keys. As I approach the car in the dark, I put my hand on the roof and insert the key in the lock. For a moment the touch of the car feels like my God. I can reach out and touch it. It is comfortingly concrete and tangible—God as a Honda Accord.

I am heading north on the New York State Thruway on my way to pick up our daughter, Susanna, from Hamilton College. The buds on the spring trees glisten in the warm, early morning sun. Somehow, my soul quickens, and a deep sense of beauty returns to my life. My fear of abandonment seems like it belongs to the past. Around Exit 16, I come to a startling new awareness that I cannot live without God. Perhaps some people are able to do that, but I know I cannot do it. I have reached the bottom, and I know clearly that I need God.

"Lord, I invite you into my life."

The Benedictine Experience

Here I am at Holy Cross Monastery, where I have been coming for retreats and spiritual direction for some eight years. The Benedictine Experience is about to begin. As evening settles in, I feel ill at ease, trapped, alone, isolated, and filled with the old fear. I don't know the others who are on this retreat. These are the same feelings as I had at Gilead a month ago. I meet in the early afternoon with Brother Douglas, who suggests that I have overly privatized my struggle and that I need to share what has happened with others.

"God is wanting to show you love through other people, in community." He tells me that what has been happening is of great importance, moving me into a far more serious spiritual journey. In the morning we are locked in with fog and can't see the lower field or the Hudson River just below. The fog seems analogous to my spiritual journey. Somehow I *know* that the river is there and that there are hills, trees and buildings on the landscape, yet it is all obscured. I'm just showing up for life in this community, not deliberately working on anything. There are fourteen of us on this retreat—a real salad bowl mix!

Betty, a retired priest's wife, seems confused by life. She fits the image of an old-fashioned clergy wife—dowdy, with little spirit or originality.

Helen, who works at the Smithsonian in DC, lives in her head and acts like a human computer.

Harvey, a cultured former Bostonian who went to the right schools, including Harvard, suddenly left a powerful corporate position in New York City to deal with his alcoholism. He divorced and moved upstate, where he bought an eighteen-thousand-acre farm and married a local teacher. He has a delightful, devilish Irish humor.

Rosemary works for the federal government. She has an air of snobby sophistication that barely covers her insecurity. She loves to drop names: "When I spoke to the people at the CIA … The Secretary of State once said to me …" etc.

Ordando, a priest from Dayton, Ohio, is studious and rather humorless. He sports a big, black, ratty beard and dresses like Daniel Boone, in lots of leather, including a burned, inscribed belt that seems to be a permanent part of him.

Rose, an elderly woman, keeps looking at those next to her out of the corner of her eye as if to correct them or ask, "What are you thinking just now?"

Janie is an overweight woman in her forties, friendly and soft-spoken. She is very self-conscious while reading the lessons in chapel, but there is a gentleness about her.

Bob, a noisy contradiction, is so liberal that he asked the Prior if he thought it was true that the CIA assassinated Thomas Merton! He is rebellious and angry and was recently turned down for the priesthood.

Fred, a radiologist from Atlanta, is studying to be an Episcopal priest. He is a very introverted, shy fellow.

Sandy is divorced and living with Bob. Their relationship is a source of tension and anxiety. She is a perennial struggler who enjoys announcing to the group, "I feel outside of this group." I find her thoughtful, sad and confused.

Will is an unusual young man with a blond beard and slight build. He is one of the most naturally undefended, spontaneous persons I have ever met; He is married, has two children, and runs a retreat/conference center in Florida. I find him a very healthy, mature, wise man.

Larry and Mary are married and come from Philadelphia. He was an accomplished scientist who almost died from a brain aneurysm and has since been somewhat impaired. He has a great sense of humor and is very friendly. Mary is a co-dependent, just recently discovering her abusive background. She is a lawyer, a strong woman who feels weak. They have seen their son go through the throes of addiction and finally get into treatment two years ago. She is growing in Al-Anon and is a lovely person.

Coming Together

In the next few days, I discover my place in this richly-textured community and begin sharing openly of my recent journey and loss of faith. Betty is unusually supportive and breaks my stereotype of her. She seems to understand the authenticity of my struggle. Bob had the usual "fix-it" comments: "Don't be so worried. Just let it all hang out, and it will pass." Janie and even Helen are most supportive and say that they are a bit envious of my struggle because it seems to have a passion that they envy. Larry is very perceptive and shares with me what the Exodus writer says about Moses, "Moses drew near to the thick darkness where God was" (Exodus 20:21). I am beginning to enjoy our group times together, feeling a sense of belonging and of being taken seriously. I sense many in the group are able to identify with my struggle. Before our morning work project, I take several from our group down to the monastery crypt to visit the tomb of Father Huntington, the founder. For some reason we begin to laugh and soon find everything hilarious—every movement, word, and gesture. Later, at Compline in the chapel, we cannot look at each other for fear of being out of control. At dinner we are told that there will be a special guest, the Prior of the monastery in Ghana, who will speak to us. At 8:00 PM, as we gather in the refectory, we see him carry an easel into the room. We glance at each other, not believing that we are in for a formal lecture. Father Abbal, a tiny, rather serious but very dedicated monk, begins by saying, "We run piggeries." When Bob asks what kind of pigs they have, several of us go over the edge. I try to focus intensely on the rotating ceiling fan. The group is barely respectful but does keep from being totally out of control. I crawl into bed at ten o'clock still laughing. Several hours later I wake myself up in hysterical laughter. For the remainder of the week, our group is free, honest, open, and filled with humor. We have become a real community, and I belong.

Love Has Won!

As I drive home from the monastery, I realize that many of the pieces of my life are being healed. I have broken the back of the anger toward my father and am ready to live my own life, releasing him from my demands. I am in charge of my own life; nothing is holding me back. I am free to live *my* life now, without excuses. My father has been restored to merely being my father, who did his best and who provided well for me. He died six months after my time in the monastery, and my mother died three months after that. As I stood on the hillside of the Maine cemetery burying my mother, I thought of Jesus' final words on the cross, and I quietly formed them on my own lips, "It is finished, it is completed." Finished is my work to resolve my relationship with each of my parents. Finished are their work and their lives on this earth. They are free and at peace and I am free and filled with resolution, and deep gratitude. LOVE HAS WON!

Freedom to Question

After my crisis of faith, I realize that I am much less proscriptive about God and much more in love with God. God is more mysterious and less prone to being easily categorized and stamped with a label. I feel like I have been shaken loose of stereotypes and neat formulas and have been introduced to the Real God; doubt has become an integral part of believing. Novelist Flannery O'Connor understands the importance of doubt: "I don't know how the kind of faith required of a Christian living in the twentieth century can be at all if it is not grounded on the experience of unbelief."[2]

I remember leading a four-week adult Christian education course many years ago. A young man, David, outgoing and popular in the parish, held back and sat on the fringe of the group. I asked each person to share what he believed. Almost everyone spoke of their doubts and uncertainties. When I came around to David, he said, "I'm hiding in this group. I deliberately came late because I thought I was the only one with doubts. I have just listened to the rest of you, many who are pillars of this church, and you are filled with doubts. In fact, you believe less than I do!" Everyone laughed. The popular assumption is that most people in the pews have it all together and never experience doubt. Author Madeleine L'Engle says that to ask the right questions is far more important than coming up with the right answers. I believe that parishes, at their best, are places where people are given permission and the freedom to plumb the difficult questions about life, evil, suffering, and God with immunity and support. The Church has its creeds and a few essential beliefs that it holds. It is, however, important for us to be honest and open in our inquiry and free to wrestle with these "essentials." This freedom will allow us to be drawn deeper into the presence of God, not being force-fed with "the correct food." I believe that faith is contagious and is passed on more through attraction than through promotion. As Christians, we have far more in common with a struggling atheist or agnostic than we do with a know-it-all, dogmatic, self-righteous believer. We all, as human beings, share the search in common.

I have met many people whose life experiences have led them to serious doubt in the reality of a loving God. Who am I as a Christian to criticize them for their difficulties with faith or their doubts? All I can do is be witness to the reality of God in my own life and help them to honor their doubt.

I have a friend who has every reason to doubt the goodness of God. Harriett, born in the Southwest, was molested by both her father and mother, who were considered outstanding citizens in their small city. She has never been able to trust, becoming promiscuous as a teenager and later becoming an alcoholic and drug addict. Her journey has been a long and difficult one; she has taken care of her parents in their failing years, gone into recovery, and married a wonderful man who understands and accepts her, including her wounds. Who would want to press Harriett to accept a prepackaged belief system? Faith has come to her as people have shared the reality of God in their own lives with her. No pressure, only love and acceptance, led her to a deeper understanding of the goodness of God as something other than a shadow of her abusive parents.

Blessing the Pain

At St. Barnabas Church, my first funeral was for the fourteen-year-old son of a dedicated parish couple. Anne and Ed are devastated, having found Todd, their young son, dead of an apparent brain aneurysm early one morning. Their faith is shaken, and they withdraw for several months. The most difficult comments for them come from well-meaning Christians who say things like, "God needed another angel in heaven," "It was Todd's time to go," and "God is testing you to make you more faithful." They and I find such comments vulgar and suggestive of an image of God as dangerous and capricious. I tell them that I don't understand Todd's death at all, but I don't believe for a minute that his death was the will of God. This allows me to be in a meaningful and trusting relationship with them and to listen with compassion to their doubts. One of the church's greatest sins is providing glib answers to life's tough questions. Sometimes, I believe, doubt purifies the search and makes us more honest. Rowan Williams, the Archbishop of Canterbury, says, "The dark night is God's attack on religion."[3] Well, that statement, from none other than the truth-telling Anglican leader, should keep things in perspective for those of us in the Church! Doubt keeps the religious institution perpetually humbled. It is a reminder that organized religion, although necessary, is not the same thing as God. Religion we can make tidy and compulsive and ever-so-sure of itself, but God—well, that's another matter! And the Archbishop has the wisdom and relationship with God to understand the difference.

Fake It Until You Make It

It was early in my ministry in New York City, and I have a parishioner who came to church every Sunday and is deeply involved in the life of the parish but cannot trust that a good God exists. It is easier for her to be an atheist than struggle with this issue. I try all the conventional ways to talk her into faith, but somehow a resistance always blocks the path. Finally Julie shares with me her abuse as a young girl. Suddenly it all makes sense. She should have difficulty in trusting God. If parents and other authority figures couldn't protect her, why would God be any different? For years she had refused to receive Holy Communion. She tells me that she would like to believe God exists but cannot bring herself to do so. I suggest that one day she might feel like going through the movements of faith without formally believing and that she might feel moved to receive Holy Communion. A couple of years, later much to my surprise, and probably to that of many in the congregation, she shyly makes her way to the altar rail and puts out her hands for the Bread of Heaven. Is this a religious moment or a secular moment? Many Christians would deem it religious. I think of it as a real moment, when God allows the pain and misconception about himself to be replaced by a moment of trust and hope. And so the journey of faith begins. Archbishop Williams continues, "The ray of darkness is not different from the dart of love."[4]

Where Love Is Found, There Is God

Sometimes God's love shines through doubt and reveals itself. Judy and I recently went to the wedding of our friends' son in South Carolina. The father, a loving, sensitive, caring man and an atheist, stands up at the rehearsal dinner and gives the most loving, genuine toast to his son and his son's fiancée that I have ever heard. Such profound love and deep feelings are shared openly. I remember the saying, "Wherever love is found, there is God." I say to Judy later, "Michael doesn't know it, but he has experienced God." St. Augustine captured the search for God, even if unnamed: "Late have I loved thee, Beauty so Ancient and so New, and behold, you were within and I apart."

The Blessings of Doubt

Contrary to popular belief among Christians, doubt and faith are not polar opposites but two sides of the same coin. Doubt is the path that explores the human issues of our lives, the dark recesses of our psyches, and the difficult experiences from our past and can lead to liberation, forgiveness, and a discovery of the presence of God behind and underneath and in the difficult stuff of our lives. Faith and doubt complement each other and make our journeys authentic. Author, Philip Yancey knows this: "Doubt is the skeleton in the closet of faith and I know no better way to treat a skeleton than to bring it into the open and expose it for what it is: not something to hide or fear, but a hard structure on which living tissue may grow."[5]

Worlds collide when doubt appears on the scene, yet it can become a path to healing and to a deeper relationship with God. I discover, as I move through life, that a variety of other dragons appear on the scene also. These cannot safely be ignored; they must be tamed. Yet they too, like doubt, put faith to the test.

2

Encountering Dragons

o o o o o o o o o o o o o o o o o o o o o o o o o o o o o o o

"It was going great, and, then I got out of bed."

—*Anne Lamott*

"Open your life to God and your life will be changed. You don't always get to say how."

—*Barbara Crafton*

The Hideous Celebration

The sexual abuse of children is casting a dark cloud over the Church and is, certainly, one of the fearful dragons that the Church must deal with proactively and directly.

It was a beautiful, late September day at St. Barnabas and the occasion for a diocesan regional assembly, with representatives from fifty parishes gathering to celebrate our common life together and to receive encouragement and vision from Bishop Paul Moore. He was joined by his suffragan bishop, Stewart Wetmore, and his wife Frances. This was a wonderful opportunity to hear our relatively new bishop set forth his hopes and dreams for the diocese for the days to come.

The celebration was grand, with some 250 people making their way in a parade down Main Street in Irvington with colored banners waving in the breeze, culminating in a glorious service in the church with a combined choir. This was a perfect occasion that had generated a great deal of enthusiasm and excitement.

As the people left and headed home, both bishops and Frances Wetmore came to the rectory for an early dinner. We had a pleasant unwinding from the celebration, sharing stories as our daughters added their two cents' worth to our conversation. Our guests loved chatting with them and made them feel a part of the festivities.

During the cocktail hour, we discovered that we needed more ice, so I went to the parish kitchen to scoop us a bowl for the party. As I approached the darkened kitchen, I heard a deep voice speaking softly, saying, "You aren't going to tell your parents, are you?" As I walked into the kitchen, I discovered the scene that no one ever wants to witness. Eddie, the sexton (custodian), was molesting a five-year-old girl, who began crying when she saw me and said, "Eddie did nasty things to me." Her parents had brought her back to the church to pick up a sweater she had left behind. They were waiting in their car in front of the church. I took the child to her parents and told them what had happened, assuring them that I would immediately deal with Eddie and call the police.

Eddie was thirty-five, a bear of a man who spoke with a thick German accent. I had inherited him when I became rector in 1972. He lived a few villages north of us with his wife, son, and daughter. Early in my tenure in the parish, altar guild women came to me and told me how uncomfortable they were being in the church alone with Eddie. I had become aware of his drinking problem, yet never found him imbibing on the job. I was sufficiently concerned to raise these issues with the vestry (board). We would be vigilant and on guard but decided that no action could be taken unless we had more specific behavior to address.

The parents took their child home to bathe her and calm her. I returned to the church to confront Eddie, who was drunk and mumbling to himself. At that moment I experienced a rage I had never felt before and have not felt since. If I had carried a gun, I have no doubt that I would have killed him in a flash. Some thirty-three years later, I still have the same feeling. Shaking, I finally said to Eddie, "You're fired. Get out of here immediately and never, never come back, do you understand?" He grunted something that made no sense and left the building.

I returned home to tell the house guests what had happened. Bishop Moore and Bishop Wetmore expressed concern but then continued the conversation as if nothing of consequence had happened. Frances Wetmore was the one who grasped the import and horror of what the child had just been through and later was the only one who called us to ask how she was doing.

I left the party to call the parents, who asked that I meet them the next morning. I then called our local detective in the Irvington Police Department, who came later and took statements from the parents and from me. What we soon discovered was that if charges were pressed, the child would have to appear in court with her molester, face him, and testify. To the parents, this seemed cruel and like further abuse, so they explored other options.

The following day, I went with the detective to Eddie's home to pick up his set of church keys. His wife gave them to me but indicated that she would like to talk to me privately. I gave her my phone number. She called the next day, and we worked out a secret meeting at a church near her home. She was horrified to learn of her husband's crime and expressed compassion for the child and what she must be going through. She told me that she was going to separate from her husband and seemed alarmed about the safety of her two children.

The Irvington Police department and three other departments became involved in making it abundantly clear to Eddie that if he were ever seen in Irvington again, that the consequences would be severe. I called a special meeting of our vestry the day after the attack and told them that a five-year-old child had been molested by Eddie. The parents and I decided to protect the child's identity so parishioners would not begin treating her differently or mark her as an "injured" child. How will we ever know if this was the right thing to do? The parents consulted with therapists and decided to wait and watch for symptoms of trauma and to be ready to talk with their daughter if she raised the subject of her molestation. She has had to deal with this violation throughout the years in a variety of layers and has done courageous and healing work with a number of therapists. She has gone on to become a physician and is very successful.

Within a month after my meeting with Eddie's wife, I began receiving disturbing phone calls from Eddie, sometimes in the middle of the night. "Is Reverend Homewrecker there?" There were many voiceless calls in which he would stay on the line without saying a word, then hang up. Eddie's wife called one day to say, "Eddie has taken our dining room furniture out into the back yard and has begun chopping it up with an ax, saying he is cutting you up in little pieces." A few weeks later, she called again to say that she thought that Eddie was on his way down to St. Barnabas with a gun and that he was coming after me. Needless to say, our anxiety and fear began to grow and became background noise to each day. Judy and I would wake up in the middle of the night, hear glass breaking outside, and be convinced that Eddie had just broken into the rectory. That same Christmas night, having gone to bed around 3:00 AM, we awoke to discover that thieves had pushed in a window in the living room and had gone through every room in the house except our bedrooms. The basement, attic, and front door were all wide open when we arose. It was soon after this incident that we had an alarm system installed in the rectory. Yet the phone calls continued, as did our regular calls to the police for protection. Eddie had, indeed, become a dragon who was invading more and more of our private and family life, with his roar reaching down into our deepest psychic niches.

There were many extra vestry meetings to address the seriousness of the situation we all confronted. Finally the board paid to send me to a psychiatrist to explore ways to deal with these threats. The psychiatrist made it clear that the way I had singlehandedly fired Eddie had brought all his rage into focus on me. His solution was to shift the responsibility to people more difficult to identify. A letter was sent to Eddie from the faceless vestry to tell him that "compassionate, kind, loving Father Colwell persuaded us not to prosecute you for your despicable crime. He also has insisted that we send you two weeks' severance pay, which we initially were against but have decided to do." This latter move I found repugnant, but the vestry followed through and sent the letter. Soon after that, I received a phone call during the day from Eddie, who said, "You know, I'm not going to hurt you."

I responded, "I'm happy to hear that, Eddie." That was the last word I heard from this sick, destructive man. We later learned that his wife fled with their children and that he later had a serious stroke and was in a nursing home. Only then did I actually feel safe. Even today I will not put my back to my office window at night. Post Traumatic Stress Disorder has taken a permanent place in our lives.

As is usually the case, in the days that followed, other parents began to tell me that their daughters had also been molested by Eddie. I met with these parents, but all refused to go public with what they had been able to put on a back shelf, dark as that shelf undoubtedly was. I have guilt and anguish to this day about the scars these victims have lived with over the years.

The Church has come a long way in these past three decades in being proactive and less secretive about sexual abuse. Such abuse in the church seems to be growing at a disturbing rate, yet I can say with great pride that the Episcopal Church is now quick to report such crimes to the police and that when there is corroboration, it takes swift action against clergy or other offenders. The shroud of secrecy has been removed. There is no longer any safe haven in our churches for child molesters. Guidelines for all our parishes are now firmly in place: No adult is to be alone with children or to meet in isolated places; Children are taught clear boundaries, background checks are done on all clergy and staff, and those dealing with children must attend a course on sexual abuse.

A former clergy assistant, Father Kenneth Brannon, preached a powerful sermon, "Seeing In The Dark," that poignantly suggests that we find light in the midst of darkness. "Resist the dual tendencies to live in the dark or hide from the dark," he wrote "Instead, learn to see in the dark: open your eyes, turn out the lights, and wait. With time, your eyes will adjust to the traces of God's light that shimmer throughout the universe. By this holy light, you will see the true dangers and treasures that lie all around you. Fight what needs to be fought and embrace what needs to be embraced. But do so knowing that you are moving toward God. As tough as things get, give thanks that you are seeing things clearly. For the better we become at seeing in the dark, the better we become at recognizing God's glory when it appears."[1] Finding God in the midst of darkness and frightening dragons is a key to throwing a light on evil.

Murder on a Summer Night

In the parish ministry, there are other dragons that threaten serenity and safety, and one such dragon is murder, the ultimate act of violence against life. Parishes are not immune to such a dragon.

It was a sticky early July evening in New York. I had been the Associate Rector in the parish for three years. In the Rector's absence, I received a call at 2:00 AM. The caller said, "Harry has been shot and is dead. Will you please come over right away?" The call was from the mother-in-law of the deceased, who lived near the Church. Their daughter and family lived a block from our apartment.

The street was teeming with police. After identifying myself, I was taken upstairs to the Sutters' apartment. I was told by a detective that Ella, Harry's wife, had shot her husband multiple times while he had been watching television. He took me first to the body lying on the floor of the small living room. "He's dead," the detective said, as if there were any real question. He then led me into the kitchen, where Ella was sitting at the table with head in her hands. As I put my hand on her shoulder, she looked up and asked, "Father Colwell, is Harry going to be OK?" I told her that he was dead, and she began to cry. Their son had slept over with his grandparents on this night. Ella seemed to have no memory of shooting her husband.

I later learned that Ella had purchased the rifle in her name three weeks before the murder. As I sat with her in the precinct house in Harlem, she seemed bewildered, numb, and blank about the entire evening. I later learned that she had called the police about thirty minutes before I arrived on the scene to say, "I just killed my husband." I spent the entire night with her at the station house talking about her child, about Harry's job, and about her nursing job at the hospital. After she was formally booked, I went home, puzzled and disturbed by the whole scene. How could I make any sense out of Ella's denial and seeming amnesia?

In the days that followed, I went to visit her once a week at the Manhattan Women's House of Detention in Greenwich Village. She told me stories of fear and abuse and that she had purchased the rifle for protection. Within a few months, Ella was able to collect Harry's life insurance and to hire a top lawyer, who eventually negotiated five year's probation.

Ella's denial puzzled me for several years. I now believe that the act of murder was so traumatic to her that she detached from its reality in her mind and disassociated from what she had done, a kind of stepping outside of one's mind to protect sanity. In later years I remembered Ella Sutter when I contemplated killing Eddie. Yes, we do hold the possibility of murder in our hearts and are capable of committing such an act. It is important to realize that it is only as we allow our darker nature to be brought out into the light that the impulses are tamed by love and the grace of God begins to inhabit our house. Did Ella kill out of fear and rage? What would have happened if she had been able to share her plight with another human being? We'll never know about Ella, but I think of her often and hope that she no longer feels trapped and has been able to let the light shine on her darkness. As the Psalmist prayed in Psalm 80, "Show the light of your countenance, and we shall be saved." Even our dark side can be baptized by the Grace of God.

Craving: The Dragon of Addiction

So they ate and were well-filled for he gave them what they craved; but they did not stop their craving, though food was still in their mouths.

—(Psalm 78:29-30)

When I was in high school, only the marginal teenagers drank and smoked; other drugs wouldn't appear on the scene for another fifteen years. My father and most men of my childhood smoked pipes, cigarettes, and cigars, yet I didn't smoke until I was in college. My parents were occasional social drinkers. My mother's father was from a German background, so recipes for making *Weiner schnitzel*, beer, and dandelion wine were inherited family sacraments. I don't remember my parents having too much to drink or spending much time thinking about alcohol, but I do remember my great-grandfather Colwell, who had been a crusty old sea captain and had developed diabetes. He had a wooden leg, which he would let me unhook so he could sit down. He also would allow me to take a sip of his beer. I idolized him. When I was thirteen or fourteen, my parents would allow me to have a sip of their drinks as well as on later camping and hunting trips. No one was ever drunk, and alcohol was associated with social, warm family occasions.

In college, however, during my first year, I discovered drinking in order to get high. On one occasion my freshman year, living in a dormitory, I drank a six-pack of beer and ran naked through Corbett Hall and visiting everyone, including my cousin, who lived on the second floor. I don't think that he was too happy to claim me as a blood relative that day. It was while at the University of Maine that I learned how to depressurize from a stressful week by spending Saturday nights at Pat's Pub in Orono. Many of us were underage, and rarely did we get "carded" At some point during my four years of college, the object of drinking shifted from socializing to getting drunk. It was a fine line that I stepped over, but once on the other side, it seemed normal to get high. Having come from a high school graduating class of twelve to a university class of a thousand, I discovered that alcohol made me less anxious and more confident. Very few students had cars in the mid 1950s, so we never drove while under the influence—we walked. The weekend partying continued throughout my four years of college.

I had felt a growing call toward the ordained ministry during these years and was deeply influenced by the Episcopal chaplain, Father Ted Lewis, and his wife Betty. In 1960 I graduated from college and entered the General Theological Seminary in New York. I packed a bottle of rum in my belongings as a "friend" I could count on as I went off to an urban, foreign environment. Surely this secrecy was a telltale sign of problems to come. Drinking in seminary was seen as a sophisticated event. Sherry (really bad, cheap, bottom-line) became the mark of a classy clergyman-to-be. There would be treks uptown to the Gold Rail Bar near Columbia University or to the famous McSorley's Bar in Greenwich Village, but the staple became the before-chapel sherry hour.

Upon graduation and ordination, I went to work as an assistant at St. Margaret's Church in the South Bronx, living on the seventeenth floor of a city housing project. I lived there alone for a year before getting married in 1964. It was there that drinking alone began to establish itself as a habit. I could settle down for an occasional evening with "my friend," who had now become a very dry martini. There was no one to measure how much I drank, so I began to consume two or three martinis on frequent occasions.

I met Judy in my last year in seminary. A classmate arranged for a blind date. Judy was living in an Episcopal residence for women in graduate school, Windham House, while at Columbia University's School of Social Work. We came from similar backgrounds and fell in love rather quickly.

Judy and I were married in August 1964 and went on our honeymoon to St. Croix in the Virgin Islands, where many parishioners from St. Margaret's had relatives. A few days after we had arrived on this idyllic isle, with the sound of steel drums and the smell of honeysuckle in the air, we met up with friends from New York who were also on their honeymoon. We went to a beachfront club where there were rum punch drinks with little plastic mermaids hanging on the glasses. I decided I needed a collection of these trinkets to take home, so I consumed about a dozen drinks. Soon after, I tried to direct the steel band; the problem was that my legs were severely compromised, and I had difficulty standing upright. On the way back to our island paradise, we were invited to have drinks with other guests from New Jersey. It took me two days to recover from the ensuing hangover. On the third day, I was to celebrate the Eucharist as a guest priest at the local Episcopal church. My head was less than clear.

In early married life, a set cocktail hour was very common. Martinis were our forte. Judy was a psychiatric social worker at a residence for emotionally disturbed children in Brooklyn and had to take six trains to get to the Jackson Avenue stop on the subway in the Bronx where we lived. The cocktail hour didn't begin until seven thirty, and we often ate as late as 10:00 PM. Both of us had high-pressured, stressful jobs and took time over drinks to share our days with each other. For me, these evening drinks became a necessity, while Judy had a much more casual attitude. She could easily skip a night. For me, that was totally unacceptable and made me anxious and upset. The casual drink had become a necessity. I had worked as a seminarian for two years at St. Margaret's and then continued as a priest for three years. By 1967 I wanted to explore the possibility of chaplaincy work, so I left the parish and spent a year in a clinical pastoral education program, working at a large state mental hospital, Rikers Island Prison, and Bellevue Hospital Center. On the weekends I was chaplain to the Orange County Jail and to a large homeless shelter about sixty miles north of New York City. At the end of this intense year, I realized that I was cut out to be a parish priest and not a chaplain. I thrived on long-term relationships and the variety of tasks a parish offers.

In 1967, we moved to the Upper East side of Manhattan, where I became Associate Rector of the Church of the Holy Trinity on East 88th St. We were generously entertained by many wonderful parishioners as well as by Clarke and Wendy Oler, my wise boss and his lovely wife, and a cocktail hour was the norm. It was in this setting that my drinking picked up steam. I began to sneak drinks and to refresh my glass before it was empty, which I did not count as an additional drink. My "friend" alcohol had become a secret partner, concealing the real truth from myself as well as from Judy and others. In 1967 our daughter Emily was born. We were thrilled to have a child, yet our lives were very stretched, and alcohol became a relaxing agent for me.

One day Judy said to me, "I don't think that we need to drink every night." I remember the panic I felt inside. I agreed, though, and we stopped the evening cocktails. I prepared meals a couple of nights a week and began trying to find reasons to prepare Italian dinners that needed burgundy to make the meal complete. We had an occasional argument about this. I began an inner dialogue that was fueled by anger because I was being deprived of my friend alcohol. When we did occasionally drink, I couldn't get enough and grew argumentative and edgy. As I look back, I realize that depression had become an element in this scene. The obsession with alcohol, the deprivation, and the anger were all destructive elements intruding themselves into our marriage. As the years passed, I found my job challenging and rewarding and my relationships with Judy and Emily, our daughter, exciting but stressful. My "friend" alcohol, however, was increasingly demanding a central place in my life.

Our second, daughter, Susanna, was born in 1971. Judy was doing well in her career and now worked only a few blocks from our apartment, having helped her agency relocate from Brooklyn to a new building on the East Side of Manhattan. I remember my genuine excitement about having a wife and two daughters I dearly loved. Family filled me with great pride, yet my friend alcohol was intruding into my closest relationships. What had been a supportive, comforting, relaxing agent was, in fact, turning me into an edgy person with a short fuse.

After five wonderful years at Holy Trinity and eight years as an assistant priest, it was time for me to have a parish of my own. We moved to Irvington, a suburb on the Hudson River, only twenty miles from midtown Manhattan in the spring of 1972. Amanda, our long-awaited, youngest daughter, was born three years later. Judy worked part-time in a number of mental health clinics in Manhattan and began a small private psychotherapy practice on the side. I loved my new job as rector of St. Barnabas, but the learning curve was sharp, involving negotiating parish politics, pastoral, and financial needs; establishing a vision for the parish; and challenging it to grow spiritually. My drinking, always quiet and private, never a public issue, continued to infect my relationship with Judy and our girls. I often felt misunderstood, moody, and resentful, as if I were not receiving enough attention. My relationship with Judy began to include very bumpy stretches. I was often very critical and angry with her, which led to her feeling unappreciated and prepared for the next attack. Even though I spent a lot of time with our children, attending all of their concerts and games, I often had a short fuse and was impatient. By 1978 this reached a breaking point, and Judy and our children were all aware of my negativity. Judy kept telling me that my drinking was an issue. In fact, in the back of my mind, I had come to realize that alcohol was at the heart of most of our conflicts and that "cutting back" or moderation would not work; abstinence was the only answer. I decided to stop drinking that winter. The decision was made after a long dialogue with God, who had led me to realize that I had to stop drinking for good, which I did in November of 1978. I was very happy and felt free, realizing what a relief it was not to be obsessed with thoughts of alcohol from the morning until I went to bed at night. This new lease on life lasted for perhaps a year; then my resentment, depression, and anger intensified. I subjected my family to this erratic, negative behavior for the next eight years, dry but far from sober. During part of this time, I had been in therapy but the drinking was never addressed. Finally Judy began to talk of separation, saying that she wasn't willing to live with my attitude any longer. I became desperate because, in spite of all of my self-justification, I knew the problem lay in me and secretly hated myself, yet could find no answer.

One day at the lunch table Judy asked, "How would you define an alcoholic?" I thought for a moment and answered, "Someone who can't control his use of alcohol." Seized by a sudden realization, I said, "I think I have just called myself an alcoholic. I meant an alcoholic who no longer drinks but still has the illness and the sick attitudes that accompany addiction, but has never addressed these or the underlying issues in any therapeutic way.

Soon after this incident, as I was thumbing through one of Judy's therapy magazines, I saw an advertisement for the Caron Foundation treatment program in Wernersville, Pennsylvania. This program seemed to address my issues. I called them on the phone and described my background and told them that I had stopped drinking eight years before but was now feeling desperate. I truly loved my family and was now willing to do anything to save it. The woman from Caron assured me that their program was for people like me, but that there was a waiting list of six months. I told her that I couldn't survive for that long, and she promised to put me on a waiting list. The next day she called to say that a cancellation had occurred and that because of my desperation, she had taken the liberty to move me up on the list. The next opening would be in three weeks. I was overjoyed, hopeful, and terrified.

On Columbus Day weekend of 1986, I went with Judy and our girls to our Fire Island family house. I left on Sunday morning and drove seven hours to Caron. There were a number of rules that would affect the week's stay: no phone calls, no books or magazines, no radio, TV, or tapes, and no medications including aspirin, unless dispensed by the staff. I wrote in my journal a few hours before leaving for Caron, "I am filled with dinner, but I'm starving to death. I feel so alone, different, and unacceptable. At work I feel abused, alone, empty, and angry."

Caron was a turning point in my life! In seven days I felt understood and accepted in a community with eleven others in a manner that I never imagined possible. I was able to be open, honest, and undefended, to be embraced by other broken and desperate people. I came to understand the loneliness of my childhood, my love affair with alcohol, and all of the characteristics of addiction as a disease: lack of gratitude, irritability, anxiety, resentment, defensiveness, self-absorption, anger, guilt, fear, isolation, entitlement, and the feeling of being different from others. It was at Caron that I discovered there was a name for what I had suffered for years and had inflicted upon Judy and my girls: alcoholism. The fact that there was a label for my experience was a liberating discovery. In the five hours it took me to drive home, I cried as I gave thanks for my new understanding. I began attending a weekly Caron group meeting in New York as well as regular meetings of Alcoholics Anonymous. AA literally saved my life. I threw myself into four or five meetings each week, got a sponsor, worked the steps of the program, shared more honestly than I had ever done before, and experienced an acceptance and a daily way to live life and to make amends for past and present behavior. It was in AA that I discovered a community of honest and broken people who had discovered hope for the future. I remained in AA for seventeen years and finally discovered that other avenues provided me with the food and the support that I needed to continue the journey of true sobriety and responsible living. In spite of my enthusiasm about recovery, my family, although thoroughly supportive, maintained that "actions speak louder than words." As the years went by, they came to see that I was, indeed, different and easier to live with. Life had become better for all of us. I will always regret my behavior before recovery but will never forget the *amazing grace that saved a wretch like me*.

Rowan Williams gets it right: "The light is at the heart of the dark, the dawn breaks when we have entered fully into the night."[2] In Psalm 139:12, the Psalmist echoes this theme: "The darkness is no darkness with thee: the night is as clear as the day." God was there in the dark depths of my addiction, calling me back to sanity and freedom and love. The dawn has broken at the heart of my darkness, and I am still filled with a profound sense of gratitude. For me it wasn't in the institutional halls of religion that I discovered freedom but in the *secular* palace of those who knew about the effects of addiction. There I met God anew, in all his generous love. I will spend the rest of my life remembering the damage I have inflicted upon Judy and our daughters and how important our relationships and love are. That is the only way I can make amends. Sometimes I wonder why I didn't come to my senses and why my turning point didn't happen twenty years earlier. I don't really have an answer other than to say that I needed to be taken to the edge of destruction so that I might see the light of God's presence in the midst of brokenness and self-righteousness. I most regret, however, pulling my family into the darkness with me. I will always be grateful for their love and faithfulness, for reflecting the incredible love that God is. There would be, however, years later, another unexpected bout with addiction.

The Dilaudid Hook

The Dilaudid chapter came uninvited and threatened to take over my life. In 1997 I was having great difficulty walking on my right foot. The muscles and tendons had collapsed, and I was literally walking on the side of my foot. Flat feet ran in my family but became most pronounced in my genes. Most orthopedists refused to do the required reconstructive surgery because it would be experimental, with no guarantees, and the threat of a lawsuit frightened them. Dr. Martin J. O'Malley of the Hospital for Special Surgery finally agreed to take on my case, which has been written up in the professional literature. The foot would be rebuilt in a six-hour surgery using harvested pelvic bone. The surgery went well but was very difficult. Bone pain is extreme, and the extensive surgery in my case required large amounts of Dilaudid, a powerful synthetic morphine that I took for a month. Afraid of becoming hooked on the drug and hating its dulling effects on my brain, I tried to cut back or skip a dose. The pain would get out of control, so I continued to take the drug until, thirty days later, the pain suddenly ceased. Upon the suggestion of the visiting nurse, I stopped the Dilaudid. Within two hours I was flooded with anxiety, dropping blood pressure, stomach cramps, diarrhea, and headaches as well as the paralyzing sense of impending doom that is an anxiety attack. It took several days to realize that I was having physical withdrawal symptoms. I had never felt any euphoria from the painkillers, so there was no psychological need for the drug. However, the nerve receptors in my brain needed the drug to feel normal, and without it they went into demand mode. I thought I was losing my mind; I couldn't carry on a logical thought process like reading and comprehending the headlines in the newspaper or on television, having no power of concentration. Judy was wonderful. She helped me to find a psychiatrist whose specialty was addiction. He slowly began to ease me off the drug, which took six months to accomplish. These were some of the most intensely depressing and difficult days I have ever endured, weeks of utter hopelessness and anxiety. I couldn't pray or sleep or even hope, but was trapped by darkness and dread. I made this journal entry:

> "You come uninvited and expand your
> presence into every room of my pained life.
> How dare you? Who are you? How familiar you try to be!
> You act as if you have always lived here with me.
> You suggest we are married and are inseparable.
> Nothing could be so false!
> For I do not know you, you bastard!
> You sneaked through my back door and
> took up residency.
> "We are together for life," you say.
> Want to bet? You are a stranger in my house.
> Your time is approaching destruction.
> You will soon be evicted.
> Then I will clean my house and open the windows
> to let the fresh air and sunshine pour in.
> Thank you, Lord, that I know the outcome.
> Dilaudid—you are going to die!"

Judy and the psychiatrist walked with me and helped me begin to see light once again. I came to realize that life can be brutally and dangerously effective in its ability to pierce our personal defenses. In the midst of my darkest time, I asked, "Will this ever end? Will I ever walk again? Will I ever get off the Dilaudid? Will God ever speak to me again?" Then I read the Gospel for that Sunday. It was the story of Elijah, the great prophet of Israel, escaping from Queen Jezebel. He traveled all the way from Beersheba down to Mt. Sinai through the desert, nearly two hundred miles. In I Kings 19:12, God says to Elijah, "Go and stand on the mountain because I am about to pass by," which Elijah does. A great and powerful wind tore through the mountains but the Lord was not in the wind. Then an earthquake rumbled through but the Lord was not in the earthquake. Then a fire came but the Lord was not in the fire. After the fire, a still, small voice," the voice of God.

I came to realize that God had been speaking to me quietly, not in the way I had demanded and wanted but from within, in a gentle whisper: "I am here." I realized that my powerlessness was my prayer, which allowed God to reach me. No illusions of strength, no false gods, no pretense of my own willpower, no hope left that I could make it all work out. It was in the desert that I discovered angels. I was being severely tempted to embrace my hopelessness, my immobilizing fear, and the apparent absence of God. In fact, powerlessness was the vehicle through which God entered my life. It is the holiest prayer we can offer. It is potent!

The dragon of addiction has become a centerpiece of my story, but there are other difficult issues that most people have to face in adulthood. The decline of parents is such an issue.

Parental Sunset

I was an only child, though not because my parents planned it that way. After a miscarriage my mother could no longer conceive. I grew up on the coast of Maine, in a small town, Hancock, known as a popular summer colony. One of the locals was Pierre Monteux, the famed conductor. It was also the location of Operation Magpie, the plot to land German spies on the deserted coast one mile from our house on November 29, 1944. This was reported to the FBI by a good friend, a high school student, who saw the spies walking on a deserted road shortly after coming ashore from their submarine.

In 1947 my father and uncle opened a wholesale lobster business, Colwell Brothers, in Stonington, about fifty miles from Hancock. This was an idyllic Island in Penobscot Bay with a population of some 2500 people, in the middle of the rugged Maine coast. My childhood was blessed with frequent, large, extended-family picnics and lots of friends who came for dinner: artists, musicians, writers, physicians, and clergy. We visited my grandmothers regularly, and my maternal grandmother lived with us in the winter. I never knew either of my grandfathers, who had died, one before and the other soon after I was born. There were wonderful camping trips, concerts, lectures, and trips to Ohio to visit my aunt and cousins. In high school I was president of my class, played trumpet in the band, and traveled all over the state of Maine for parades and contests. I played in a dance band and acted in most theatrical productions in high school. When older, my cousin Dick and I worked on the docks every summer, unloading boats of herring and mackerel. We bought lobsters from local fishermen, sold bait and gasoline, and loaded trucks with crates of lobsters to be transported to Boston. It was a magical childhood, filled with culture, hard work, and family—I have thirty-two first cousins. I enjoyed time with friends, church youth groups, raising chickens, and riding my bicycle up and down the steep island hills. I was raised as a Congregationalist but became a Methodist in the absence of any Congregational Church when we moved to the island. I became interested in the Episcopal Church through family summer friends during my senior year in high school.

I left home for the University of Maine in 1956 and began to discover a broader world. I was confirmed in the Episcopal Church the next spring. My mother had some difficulty allowing me to spread my wings and to become an adult. I began to understand how enmeshed her world was with mine and found it necessary to put some distance between us. When I almost failed my first year in college, my mother's comment was, "I don't know how you *do* as well as you do." This was countered by my father's crisp, "You'd damn well better shape up and work harder!" I actually appreciated his advice and understood it as more respectful of my abilities. In college I fell in love with a young woman and rarely went home, much to my mother's distress.

I graduated from college in 1960, went on to New York to the General Theological Seminary, and then continued to live in New York, where I was married a year after being ordained. Although outwardly supportive of my new wife, my mother had a difficult time accepting Judy because she saw her as competition. She dearly loved our daughters and Judy also, but at the same time she was never quite able to appreciate and accept that we were a separate family.

Fast forward to 1989. My mother, who had had been crippled from birth from a common hip dysplasia that was not treated, was now suffering from severe arthritis and high blood pressure. She finally had a very serious, disabling stroke and was placed in a nursing home on the island, a truly progressive and humane place where she knew the whole staff and found comfort and support.

My father was distraught to have lost his companion and dearest friend and spent every day with her, but he wasn't able to take care of himself or to eat properly. He was becoming senile and losing weight and finally had a minor stroke himself. We realized that it would be necessary to move both parents to New York, where my mother would be in a nearby nursing home and my father would live with us. This was an extremely disorienting and difficult move for them. My mother spent the first six months saying that she wanted to go back to her home in Maine, denying her severe paralysis and dependency. My father would drive himself the three miles to the nursing home each day, spending eight hours with my mother. The strain on him was obvious; he began to develop congestive heart failure, and his senility worsened.

During this time I had planned to take a six month sabbatical, the first and only one I have ever taken. My base would be home, with a few short courses of study over the months. In many ways this plan was fated, because the pressure of caring for both parents was enormous. Judy really went the extra mile with both my parents, being loving, nurturing, kind, thoughtful, and sensitive. And our daughter Amanda, then fourteen years old and the only child at home, was incredible with both my parents. For me, however, it was a different story. I found a tremendous anger surfacing, irrational and disturbing. As I mentioned previously, my father had been absent as a guiding figure for much of my childhood, first in his role as a sea captain and then as a businessman who often worked fourteen hours a day. Suddenly the roles were switched: I had become the father, and my father was the child. I found this enraging, stoking my anger.

On sabbatical I spent much time at home, but it was a mixed blessing. My mind was always preoccupied with the responsibilities of caring for my parents, and I began to feel trapped by circumstances. My mother ran out of money halfway through the first year in the nursing home, which meant filing reams of paperwork to apply for Medicaid. My father, a math wizard, suddenly couldn't keep his checkbook straight. He would have an occasional outburst at the dinner table, which was unlike him. On occasion, he would smear his food all over the table. He suddenly began to skip showers and to wear the same clothes day after day. Our daughter Amanda managed him with great sensitivity and finesse. The complexities of dealing with aged, infirm parents while trying to live and work with normalcy became an immense challenge.

My sabbatical led me to my crisis of faith, triggered by my conflicted feelings about my father. When God gets his hands on our lives, tasks like caring for aged parents become grist for the mill. This period was an important one because, as a result of these final days of my parents' lives, I was able to work out my relationship with them and to finally feel at peace when they died. The word "religion" (*re-ligio*) means to reconnect and restore. I guess I found religion in those final years. Father Richard Rohr talks about Christianity as being less about addition than subtraction, getting rid of that which imprisons us and holds us back. AA certainly paved the way for me to be able to approach these sunset years with some clarity and grace. Yet the last chapter had not yet been written.

Depression as Retreat

My father died soon after Christmas in 1990 and my mother in mid-March of 1991, just three months later. I had gained insight and freedom in the last days of their lives but the work was not over. I was to struggle with a major depression for the next two years.

I love a conversation in Anne Lamott's book *Blue Shoe* about depression.

"I want to kill myself," Mattie tells Angela one night on the phone, "and get on with my life."

"Honey," Angela replies, "you don't know yourself well enough right now to commit suicide. So it would be considered a homicide."[3] In the months after my mother's death, I felt relief and gratitude that it was finally over and we could recover a normal life again. Our youngest, Amanda, was still in high school, and our other two daughters would return home from college for vacations. I was very busy in the parish and attending AA meetings several nights a week, but slowly the world began to look gray and colorless. I began to sleep late and had little energy. Then I entered that realm where I would hear myself and others as if from a distance. I became an observer of life, but a disengaged observer. Every task took extra energy; joy and excitement were faded memories. I remember sitting in parish meetings and sneaking a peek at my watch, thinking, "Only thirty more minutes before this is over." Preparing sermons and writing articles for our monthly newsletter were torturous. I had lost my enthusiasm and passion, two things I normally held in great supply; the world was flat and one-dimensional. After an AA meeting one night, I went home and told Judy, "I have just come to the realization that I'm depressed, and I think I need to get help." Judy helped me locate a psychiatrist, whom I then saw for nearly two years. In the early sessions, he zeroed in on the loss of my parents in a three-month period the prior year. I said I had resolved those relationships already. My marriage and relationship with my children had never been better. My job was in great shape, challenging and rewarding. I no longer drank. I could find nothing that could be the cause of this depression. So I began a regimen of anti-depressant drugs and would visit the shrink for a half hour once a month for drug adjustments.

In the beginning of this regimen, I felt some brief hope. The medicines would begin to work and to lift my spirits and energy for a few days and then would suddenly fail. I tried eleven different medications in a two-year period. Month after month, I would begin to hope again. Then the next medication would fail, and I reverted to a zombie-like state of barely functioning. I had great difficulty sleeping, so I took prescribed drugs to get through the night but was hung over in the morning from these sedatives.

About a year into this sinkhole, I read, in an article about depression, a theory that the psyche uses depression to reorder, process, and integrate material that needs attention. At first I cast this theory aside, but for some reason I kept returning to it.

I had a very difficult time putting one foot in front of the other, remaining pleasant and pastoral in the parish. I also found personal prayer nearly impossible. Two years after the depression's onset, I found myself in charge of a healing workshop led by the late Australian Anglican priest, Canon Jim Glennon. A fellow priest and friend, Father Bob Godley, whose parish was nearby, had been scheduled to sponsor the event but had been hospitalized after an accident. I was in charge of the event, which was to take place over several evenings in the spring. I decided to ask God to provide a sign if I was meant to ask Jim Glennon to pray for my healing. Within a couple of weeks, I began having an adverse reaction to the antidepressant. I had symptoms of overdosing, which necessitated cutting back on the drug. I remember thinking, "Perhaps this is the sign I asked for." Jim came and led the mission. I shared the fact of my depression with him and told him I was going to ask for him to pray for me to be healed at that night's service, which I did. He told me to claim my healing and get on with life. The depression lifted, and I slowly withdrew the medication and finally experienced vitality, passion, and enthusiasm once again.

Only as I began writing about this period did the words form themselves for this book, and then I understood the purpose that my depression had served. I had been totally absorbed in coping with one crisis after another, with my loss of faith on sabbatical, and with my parents. Even though I had experienced growth and a arrived at a resolution, I still needed time to stop the roller-coaster and process it all, to integrate the work I had done in my relationship with my parents. I had to face my own conflicts and irrational anger; I had to let go of my need to be the child with my parents. I was faced with love underneath the layers of guilt. My parents' greatest gift to me in their last days was to help me grow up and to realize what a blessing they had been in my life. Their sunset, although an ending for me, was also a new beginning. I now have become an adult, no longer feeling orphaned by my parents' deaths. All of this had overloaded my mental and emotional circuits, however, so that I required respite and psychic withdrawal time. I do not believe that all depressions are the same. Some seem to be purely caused by a chemical imbalance, while others are initiated by a psychological conflict or trauma. All, however, have a spiritual component that is important to honor. God was with me in the furnace, even though I couldn't feel his presence much of the time. I like what Bishop Tutu says about the presence of God in suffering: "The God we worship doesn't tell his people to wear fire-proof suits before going to the furnace. He goes right in there with them. God doesn't give us good advice from the sidelines but is there with us in the muck of life. God does not take our suffering away but he hears us and strengthens us to bear it."[4] My whole life has become the place where earth and heaven mingle and God uses flesh and psyche and the furnace of despair as portals for his love. In God's economy, nothing is wasted; everything is used for our growth and maturity and the deepening of our relationship with God.

I have spent forty-five years as a parish priest and have helped hundreds of parishioners face their own dragons. Often, however, the Church perceives the world as the enemy. The world and the ordained ministry often collide with each other, yet the ordained ministry provides an important playing field for addressing and healing this split. There are many harmful stereotypes of the ministry that need to be exposed if it is to stay focused on its message.

3

Demythologizing the Priesthood

○ ○

As a priest I am called to stand in two places at once, at the center of a particular story-telling tradition and at its edge.

—*Alan Jones*

Ministry came easier when I stopped trying so hard to be a priest.

—*Chloe Breyer*

The 96th Street Ordination

A gentle March breeze feels like a friend as I briskly walk up Madison Avenue on my way for a required psychiatric interview, two months before my expected graduation from seminary. My time there has been three years of deconstruction of my simple faith as I was exposed to higher Biblical criticism, to theories of atonement, and to a new view of Christian history, as well as to psychological challenge. Somehow I had passed my first psychiatric exam three years earlier in the Diocese of Maine to be accepted as a candidate for the priesthood. Is the message, "If you weren't unstable when you entered the hallowed walls of the General Theological Seminary, you well may be by the time you complete your three years"? Now, three years later, I feel like a person who is unfinished and unintegrated, and I think to myself, "And they think I am ready for ordination! I know less about myself than I thought I knew when I first entered seminary. Ordination? No way!" I have an image of this Park Avenue shrink looking across his desk, psychological test results in hand, condescendingly smiling and saying, "You've come a long way, Mr. Colwell, and I can see that seminary has been an important part of your journey, but I think that you will be happier being a teacher or even a social worker. I cannot approve of your advancement for ordination because all the tests indicate that you are not suited for the demanding, complex work of the priesthood."

My steps quicken as I turn onto East 96th Street, and I nervously make my way up the block and to the corner building on Park Avenue, where I am to receive my sentence. Casually I pretend to read *Time* in Dr. Goss's tiny waiting room. In fact, I am staring at the page, trying to control the butterflies and the panic that keeps surging over me like huge ocean waves. Finally the door opens, and a depressed-looking, middle-aged patient emerges, staring at the floor.

"Mr. Colwell? Come on in," says the suave, polished, kind-looking doctor. I am ushered into his well-appointed office and sit down. Dr. Goss begins by calling me "Charlie," which actually puts me at ease. "Charlie, I have reviewed all of your psychological test results from this past winter and your essay on why you want to be a priest. I also have the results of your psychiatric exam from three years ago. Before I pull it all together with you, why don't you tell me how you feel about the possibility of graduating from seminary in a few weeks and going on to ordination?"

"Well," I began, "it's been a very stretching and eye-opening three years. I think I arrived at seminary with a very simple, untested faith and had little idea of how I would have to take my life apart and reconstruct it. Seminary has affected every aspect of my being. I am working hard to integrate the different pieces, academic and psychological, and to come to some understanding of what priesthood really is, but I've not arrived yet. I feel as if I've just started." ("You fool," I berate myself, "you have just shared too much and revealed yourself as inadequate to be a priest.")

"OK, Charlie, let me fill you in on how I see you." The awful moment of truth has arrived. The shrink begins, "Charlie, you are exactly where you belong. You are doing what you have been called to do. You think you don't have it all together, and of course you don't. You're in an important process of development, and you have a great deal to offer the Church. You have brains, curiosity, motivation, and a sense of self that will serve you well in this vocation."

I sit there, stunned and overwhelmed and speechless. "Does he see something I don't see?"

On autopilot, floating along the street as if on a layer of buoyant air, I leave the building, though I won't remember walking out of there. As I walk across 96th Street toward Fifth Avenue to catch a bus downtown, I am suddenly seized by the most profound experience I have ever had: the buildings along the street are transformed into the City of God. I see into the very center of reality, which is love, and know that love is the glue that holds the universe together. Everything makes perfect sense and is integrated, even though in reality nothing has changed. I hear the words repeated, "It is good. It is good. It is *very* good." I see a clear path ahead. There is no road map, but a journey that already is God's, and that is the right path for my future. This experience remains, some forty-five years later, as real to me as it was on that March day in 1963. I believe that this event *was* my ordination, later to be affirmed and blessed by the Church. Not many can claim to have been ordained on East 96th Street in New York City, but here is where I began my priesthood. If God uses the secular and the ordinary to reach us, then a psychiatrist and that noisy, grimy, bustling street on the East Side of Manhattan became sacramental for me on that spring day. Worlds that seemed to collide an hour ago now have merged into a vision that provides purpose for my future.

Jacob's Story

There's a wonderful story in Genesis 32 about Jacob. In this story is found, I believe, a pattern for priests and those in the ordained ministry. It is a good story because it helps to keep our eyes focused on the right things and demythologizes much that is pious and distorted about ministry.

The story begins with Jacob journeying south through what is now Jordan; he comes to the Jabbok River, which runs perpendicular to the Jordan River. He sends his wives, two maids, and eleven children across the river but doesn't go with them. He probably needed a break! As Jacob sleeps that night, a man (God) wrestles with him until the break of day. Jacob apparently gives the man a run for his money. In the end, however, he is injured when his hip bone slips out of its socket. Then the man says to Jacob, "Let me go." Jacob says, "I'm not going to let you go until you bless me." The man asks, "What is your name?" He answers, "Jacob." The man says, "No longer will your name be Jacob; from now on it will be 'Israel' (God-wrestler)." The man then blesses Jacob, and Jacob names the place Peniel, "for I have seen God face to face and my life has been preserved." Jacob limps as the sun comes up and departs from Peniel. In this story Jacob *wrestles*, is *wounded*, receives his *name*, and is *blessed*. These elements become necessary ingredients for authentic ministry.

Wrestling

The priesthood is a vocation, not a profession. Jeremiah knew about vocation when he quoted God as saying, "Before I formed you in the womb I knew you as my own. Before you were born I consecrated you; I appointed you as a prophet to the nations." (Jeremiah 1:5) Years ago I had a call committee from an old, prestigious parish approach me. We entered into a lengthy process of exploration. I was clear that I felt no call from God to move but would be open to it if the process with the call committee clarified that my specific gifts were what they sought. Finally their long list of some seventy-five candidates was narrowed to two very different people. At the eleventh hour, they announced that, because the two of us were so similar, they would be making their final pick on the basis of style. Realizing that they had never engaged with the content of my ministry and what it had to offer, I withdrew my name and then received a call from my bishop, Paul Moore, Jr., whom I knew very well.

He shouted, "What have you done? Charlie, you are a goddamned fool." I responded by saying, "Thank you, Bishop, for your Godly advice." He was a wonderful man, dedicated and courageous. In this situation, however, he was thinking of the priesthood as a professional career and of that post as a necessary step on my ladder of success. I later joked with him about this incident over lunch just before he died. There is an ever-present temptation for clergy to adopt as their own the corporate world's way of moving forward, yet the clergyman who accepts this view misses the point of vocation. Archbishop Rowan Williams says it well: "Vocation is, you could say, what's left when all the games have stopped. It's that elusive residue that we are here to discover and to help one another discover."[1]

Priests are in the meaning business, helping themselves and others struggle with the core issues of human existence: life, suffering, relationships, health, and evil. What an incredible blessing it is to be allowed such intimate access to people's lives: the devastated parents of a stillborn child that the mother has carried for four months with full knowledge; another mother who is struggling with aborting a pregnancy; the phone call after the Easter service telling me that a woman has gone home to discover her husband had committed suicide with a shotgun in their bedroom; ministering to a middle aged man who is arrested for business theft; paying for heroin for a junkie in the South Bronx so he wouldn't steal anything or injure anyone the night before I was to take him to a detox unit; encouraging a woman to get psychiatric help for her serious depression; helping a man and woman face the reality of his adultery. Where else is one allowed entrance into people's lives in such depth and with such intimacy? For me, priesthood is a profound calling where, as I help others struggle with the depths of human experience, I too, am working on my own stuff.

I went to work as a priest at St. Margaret's Church on East 156th Street in the South Bronx in 1964. The local police precinct was the same one that appeared in the movie *Fort Apache: The South Bronx*. It was a black parish in the midst of a growing Hispanic area. I was the only white person in the area, living a few blocks away in St. Mary's Park Houses. I was the white person who integrated that neighborhood of three thousand families. I had worked at St. Margaret's for two years as a seminarian and desperately wanted to go there as a priest. The people were warm and open, and the challenges of the inner city called on my sense of mission and adventure. Heroin addiction was rampant, and street crime was a fact of life.

I started my ministry in the South Bronx, believing I was ready to save people. The vicar of the parish, my boss, went to Europe for his vacation and left me in charge. I immediately encountered scores of heroin addicts and a psychotic woman, a delusional parish secretary who wrote a play casting me as "the pompous puppy." We had seventeen parishioners in prison. Soon I was robbed at knifepoint by a young addict I had been helping. I began experiencing a gigantic collision between my ideals, my exalted view of priesthood, and the reality of the streets. Luther Powell, the senior warden (president of the board) and father of the former Secretary of State, Colin Powell, became my confidant and guide through these murky waters. My predecessor had told me never to show myself in the neighborhood without wearing clerical clothing. I sensed a wide and troublesome gap between how I knew myself and how others saw me. Who was I? If my parishioners really knew me, would they accept me? This was my first experience of "the Trap"—of being squeezed into a role as a priest who was separate from the world. At first I felt like a prisoner in the housing project I lived in because of my sense of this pressure to always act like a priest and not like the person I was in real life. One summer day, I left the building wearing Bermuda shorts, and the neighborhood children who usually would say, "Hello, Father," didn't recognize me without my collar. As a result of these experiences, wanting to narrow the gap between my self-image and how others saw me, I went into therapy. I have great contempt for clergymen who piously play church, who have honed the role of "priest" to that of a stereotypic sixteenth-century English vicar. When I was in seminary, I knew several fellow students who had developed English accents without ever crossing the Atlantic! I know a number of clergy whose piety gives religion a bad name, priests who never seem to forget their clerical role for a moment. They seem to push aside the fact that they are fragile, human beings like the rest of humanity, called to a specific role within the laity. I believe that priests are not a different breed from laity, nor are they more important in their role. Clergy are laity who have been called and authorized to perform special functions within that body. So a priest remains a layperson, but one with a unique role. It is important for clergy not to be more spiritual than the God who chose to live as one of us in human flesh. I remember being Spiritual Director on a Cursillo Weekend (a small, intensive course in Christianity) many years ago. I had recently had foot surgery, which necessitated my wearing white sneakers with my black cassock. A young priest approached me and said, "Father, with all due respect, I do think you should wear shoes instead of sneakers. You need to dress like a priest for this retreat." I was appalled by his rigid image of what a priest should look like and suggested that he mind his own business. These external, superficial images pale in light of the priest's awesome role of ministering to real needs and conditions and helping a group of people become honest and motivated in allowing God to lead them toward maturity, wholeness, and health.

As a clergyperson, I must wrestle (as Jacob did with the man) with the issue of being both a public and a private figure. There are two roles: living my role as a priest, saying the right things, being aware that I am an icon of God; and going home, taking off my shoes, and telling it as it really is. Over the years I have lived with a great deal of tension, swinging from one role to the other. In *Ministry Burnout*, the Jungian analyst and author John Sanford says, "Since the ministry person functions in a role in which he is handed a persona by the persons he serves, he is in danger of losing himself. But if we lose ourselves, we will also lose our energy. We will become like a watch that has lost its mainspring because we will have lost contact with our genuine self, the Center of our being."[2]

I have struggled with loneliness and isolation as a priest. It has been important for me to be involved beyond the parish in the non-church world. I have served on a volunteer ambulance corps, on the board of a foster care agency, with an organization that provides substance abuse education and training for schools and agencies, and on advisory boards of the village I live in. I have served on a myriad of diocesan committees that have provided a larger picture of the Church for me and prevented me from becoming parochial in my thinking. To counter isolation, I have organized groups of clergy who can be honest, vulnerable, and real with each other as, together, we have explored our own struggles. After being a priest for twelve years, I entered into a doctoral program at Drew University, focused on facilitating spiritual renewal in a congregation. This time as a student was a very important period in my ministry because it allowed me to have my work critiqued by other clergy and gave me the opportunity to be inspired by the work of others in similar situations. It also engaged the parish in a study that was connected with the broader Church and had implications for the wider church community.

Speaking of wrestling, parish conflict comes with the turf. It is important not to fall into the "church speak" or "sweet talk" syndrome. I don't know where people got the idea that there should be no conflict in churches. The Church is probably the devil's largest playing field. It is important for priests and other people to be real, honest, respectful, and engaged with each other. Conflict is part of life and needs to be faced before it goes underground; to avoid conflict is to postpone confrontation. Wrestling with each other, whether in a marriage, a friendship, or a parish, becomes the sacramental vehicle for the presence and grace of God; it is truly a sacred endeavor. There is no shortcut to facing conflict. The only authority we really have as clergy is earned by consent, not conferred by ordination. On the one hand, we must dare to challenge our people; on the other hand, we must love them and be sensitive pastors. This leaves little room for unilateral decisions. Moralizing and saying *you should* or *you must* doesn't work; it provokes guilt, which rarely encourages positive change. Once the Gospel is reduced to law instead of grace, all is lost. Anger from others makes me uneasy, but I have learned to deal with it head on. Often a person's anger has little to do with the issue presented and is old stuff from the person's family of origin. To help the person figure out where strong emotions originate is to award the person a mark of freedom and peace. Anger runs through life in any community, and the church certainly is not exempt. If conflict is avoided, the anger is often expressed in inappropriate places or in an oblique or covert manner and has a damaging effect on the parish as a whole. As a result of Jacob's wrestling with God, he is wounded, the second important element in priestly life.

Wounding

Back in the 60s, Judy and I had a stone tumbling machine. I remember taking a few small rocks at Fire Island and putting them in a tub that spins much like a clothes dryer. After several hours, polished, brightly colored, smooth, richly-textured objects of beauty emerged. If we had never turned on the machine, the stones would have remained dull, rough, and ordinary in spite of their potential. The prize we receive for struggling and for rubbing and bumping against each other, sometimes in a painful way, is a community that knows its identity and the price it has paid for its health. The priest and writer Henri Nouwen preached in my parish back in the 1980s. He was an impressive example of a wounded healer, (which is the title of one of his books). He talked of the wounded and the vulnerable as the ones who best experience wholeness. He spoke of making our wounds available as a source of healing. Wounding is necessary for growth to occur. If, as a priest, I am not affected by conflict and difficult times, then I am holding back from being vulnerable and open as a human being.

One of the most important tools I have come to discover for ministry is my own vulnerability. *Vulnare* means *to wound.* In many ways I am a self-protective person who has difficulty with trust. What I have come to realize is that the more I share my struggles and my attempt to integrate the various parts of myself with my parishioners, the more encouragement it gives them, the more they can identify their struggles with mine and the less isolated I am. We are, after all, engaged in the same human struggle. My struggle, as a person who is also a priest, is no more holy than the struggle of those who sit in the pews. In being vulnerable with each other, we are open to God's power. St. Paul knew about weakness, which forced him to turn to God and others to discover strength. "So, if some one wants to be a minister let him be happy to make his weakness his special boast so that the power of Christ may stay over him … for when he is weak, then is he strong." (2 Corinthians 12:9-10) My parish and I have come to know and accept each other and make some tough decisions, sometimes pushing each other beyond our comfort zones. This happens naturally as we embrace life and events together. We have struggled with issues of being more welcoming to new people, to tithing a minimum of 10 percent of the budget to outreach, to adopting the sacrament of the Eucharist as the central act of worship each Sunday, to being open to Jews and Muslims and issues such as setting boundaries for acting-out members and sex offenders.

Many years ago a couple came to the parish and began complimenting me on my sermons and the adult education courses I led, telling me how gifted I was. I fell for the praise and became their private chaplain, always available. Three years later, one night, at a parish party Bob and his wife Sally approached me to say how concerned they were that I looked so tired. I assured them that it was an unusually busy time of year and that I was just fine. Two days later Sally hand-delivered a three-page letter from the two of them, telling me that I was spiritually bankrupt and psychologically ill, that I was misleading my flock, and that I should consider leaving the priesthood. I was devastated and felt set up and attacked—which, of course, was exactly what had happened. I began to realize that my own vanity led me to this moment; I had sucked up their praise like a sponge and given Bob and Sally special treatment. I shared their letter with the vestry, and they soon left the parish. On the heels of such betrayal, I felt like never again sharing my life with parishioners; it was too dangerous. I held onto that feeling for about a month, then realized that without sharing myself with my people, I would be a mechanical, lifeless priest. The doors began to open once again. Without wounds, we have little to offer the world.

One of the tricky aspects of ministry is balancing family and priesthood. In my early life as a priest and as a newly married man, I took many wounds on this battlefield! I remember being out for meetings five nights a week, working all day Saturdays and Sundays, and asking my wife Judy to understand that I was a priest and that this calling took precedence over everything else. We had many arguments about this imbalance, but the light dawned for me one day when Judy said, "But I thought God called you to marry me as well as to be a priest." I suddenly realized mine was a dual vocation, that I didn't have to order them by importance. In subsequent years I have tried to strike a balance between work and family life. I would not be honest if I said that there are never conflicts, yet I usually know when my loyalties are out of order and move to even the balance.

A number of years ago, Judy was diagnosed with thyroid cancer. For several weeks before and after the surgery I was preoccupied with the home front. A few years later, as I have mentioned, my father and mother moved from Maine to New York in the last years of their lives. For our family these were difficult years of doctors' appointments, medical crises, endless forms to fill out, fear and anxiety about handling their end-of-life issues. During these times I needed to take a lot of time from my parish to manage their issues. On the other hand, in a six-month period, I once had five deeply involved parishioners dying. I had no clergy assistant at the time. I spent an enormous amount of time providing pastoral care to them and to their families and preparing for funerals, as well as helping the parish look at the inevitable issues of why God allows suffering and why some are healed and others are not. This was a period when I had little extra to give to my family. Knowing that family and priesthood are each vocations, calls by God, has allowed me to live with a sense of divine purpose, even though inevitably, sometimes that life is out of balance.

Naming

In the Genesis story, Jacob's name is changed only after he wrestles and is wounded. A similar pattern has led me to discover my true identity while hearing the Christian story and finding my place in it. Some of the most inspiring moments of my ministry have come from helping others wrestle and witnessing their bruises and injuries as I have walked with them on rough terrain.

Lester Graaskamp was a powerful Wall Street figure who commanded respect and fear in many people. When I arrived at St. Barnabas in 1972, he was one of the movers and shakers of the congregation. The Episcopal Church began a series of trial Prayer Books as I arrived at St. Barnabas. These were difficult times for many traditional, 1928 Prayer Book devotees like Lester. On my first Sunday, he met me at the door after the service, holding his copy of the traditional Prayer Book, waving it in my face and saying, "When you return to this book, I'll return to church!" I called Lester repeatedly over the next three years, requesting permission to sit down for a visit.

"No offense to you, Charlie, but I'm not ready yet. When I am, I will call you."

Parishioners, especially the vestry (board) and the Stewardship Committee, demanded that I "fix" the problem and bring Lester back into the fold, but my hands were tied. Finally, in 1975, Lester called.

"Charlie, I would like to see you. Will you come to my house?" I discovered that Lester had been diagnosed with terminal cancer and had been given less than a year to live. As we sat in his den, he finally made a painful confession. "I have been the backbone of St. Barnabas for forty years, and I have no idea who God is. Will you help me?"

In the six months that followed, I encouraged Lester to read the Gospels, asking him to explore how Jesus reveals what God is like. He faithfully did his homework. As I met each time with Lester to glean his thoughts, I was impressed with his childish honesty and openness to the assignment. Finally, as the end approached, Lester became afraid of dying. I suggested that he reach out and take the hand of Jesus and allow him take him to the other side. About a week later, the family called to say that Lester was dying in the hospital. I rushed to his bedside. Barely conscious, and incredibly weak as he was, I asked him how he was doing. He opened his eyes wide, looked at me, and said, "I have my hand in his." He closed his eyes and died an hour later. God had reached into Lester's tough, fear-filled, desperate heart, and Lester had made a remarkable turnaround in a short time. Somehow I knew who I was as a priest that day while witnessing God at work in Lester. My identity as a priest was clear as I served as a vehicle for and a witness to God's mighty acts. We stand in two places at once as clergy. The priest Alan Jones points out, "One of our problems is that many think they have been ordained to preach and to deal with the known rather than having been commissioned to explore the unknown. Priests and ministers have to learn to be in two places at once, spiritually speaking. They have to be grounded in the tradition of which they are the representatives. At the same time they have to be pioneers of the uncharted and unknown. They have to represent their tradition and transcend it simultaneously."[3]

Sybil, the mother of two young teenagers, had developed a virulent strain of viral pneumonia, resistant to antibiotics, and was critically ill with a high fever in a local hospital. I went to visit her as soon as I heard of her situation, but she was surrounded by her family, making it difficult for me to speak freely and to find out what she was feeling. I prayed, laid hands on her, and left. On my way home, only a twenty-minute drive, I heard God saying to me, "Turn around and go back." Brushing these words aside as a trick of my own mind, I drove on. At home I had dinner and felt the strong call once again.

I said to Judy, "I have to go back to see Sybil now." She seemed a bit surprised by this, but I left, feeling embarrassed to be doing what, on the surface, seemed irrational.

When I arrived, Sybil was alone but sitting up in bed, eager to talk. "Shortly after you and my family left, I saw Jesus standing beside my bed. His hair was golden and beautiful. He took my hand and put it on his head, and I immediately knew that my fever was gone and that I was well. Thank you for coming back. I really needed to tell you what happened." As I drove home the second time, I felt privileged to be a priest and a witness to God's healing power. That day I knew who I was, and all the money in the world could not have removed me from my calling. I thought of a scene from *The Diary of a Country Priest* that I had read in seminary: "Oh, miracles—thus to be able to give what we ourselves do not possess, sweet miracle of our empty hands."[4]

Dorothy, in many ways, was my nemesis, always critical of my ministry. After disciplining her son for his out-of-control behavior in the Sunday school, my road was a slippery slope; I could do nothing right.

"The way you pastor is a disgrace to the priesthood," she sharply reminded me one day.

Then, at forty-four, Dorothy developed acute leukemia. This mother of two young children and wife of a busy teacher called me, desperate for support and spiritual comfort. I was surprised and moved that she was reaching out to this terribly ineffective and inadequate clergyman. Over the next year, Dorothy and I became very close. There wasn't a pious bone in her body; she was a realist, yet she raised her fear with courage and persistence. She thanked me for my biweekly visits and for allowing her the room to vent her feelings. She received the Eucharist weekly and showed remarkable strength as she navigated the rocky road of temporary remission followed by an aggressive attack of the white cells in her body. The end came while I was on vacation. I drove from Fire Island to New York City to see her as she lay dying in the hospital. She told me how difficult it was to leave her husband and children, joked about what the trip to heaven would be like, and thanked me for being with her during her year-long ordeal. She died two days later. For me, it was a lesson in humility. It was important to allow Dorothy to be more than my enemy. God had reached across the chasm of ugly feelings and had brought the two of us together. A fellow priest, Robert Massie Jr., says, "The Church makes big mistakes but it is also the midwife for the birth of millions of quiet and tiny miracles of healing."[5] It is in ministering to people like Dorothy that I have discovered my true identity as a priest. In being open to her need, I moved beyond her dislike of me and witnessed God moving in her life often through my words and hands.

A clergy assistant of mine, ordained for a little more than a year, once confessed to me, "I haven't thought of myself as a priest for at least two weeks!" I assured her that this was a good thing; it meant that her priestly identity was being integrated with her person, a sign of maturity. She seemed relieved. For clergy it is tempting to split the roles between being a priest and being a private person, yet we live in a world that is claimed by God, so the artificial boundaries between secular and religious are in fact a human construct. The Rev. Fred Burnham, Director of the Trinity Institute in New York, tells Karen Armstrong, the English writer, "Karen, you always claim that you have never had a religious experience but I disagree. I think you are constantly living in the dimension of the sacred. You are absorbed in holiness all the time!"[6] It is easy for us to miss God by seeing life as ordinary when, in fact, God usually is revealed amidst the ordinary stuff of daily life. Sometimes, however, we need someone else to point this out to us. There is a popular saying, "Life is what happens when you're busy doing other things." A priest might say, "Priesthood is what happens when you are not particularly aware of being a priest."

Blessing

My years as a priest have shown me God's pattern of wrestling, being wounded, and discovering my name. All these elements from the Jacob story, however, result in God's blessing our efforts, which are often obscure in the moment and lost amidst the details. We are, like Jacob, blessed and sent out to bless others, to take the gifts we have received, and to share them. Often, however, the fruits of ministry show up decades later, and each time I am deeply moved by the way God has used a piece of my priestly work in the life of another.

"My name is Ronald Davidson. Though you would have no particular reason to remember me, I shall always remember and be thankful to you. It was in 1964 when you rescued my family and me from the depths of despair and poverty. My mother, who died in 1995, remembered and spoke of you often and fondly." This letter, received forty years after I left the South Bronx parish I had worked in, was an incredible surprise. Ron was about ten when we at the church helped his family survive after they were forced to go on public assistance. Never members of a church, they reached out to us at St. Margaret's for help and support. Subsequently, I learned that Ron had gone on to college and medical school, had taught courses at Harvard, had been the administrator of two large public hospitals in Washington, DC, and was now studying to become an Episcopal priest. "Blessed to be a blessing," as God says to Abraham. I realize that I, as a priest, can never overestimate the importance of the smallest services provided to others.

I recently received another letter from a woman, Ruth, who was raised in a terribly abusive home, had no faith, and found church a "head trip." She came to see me one day and poured out her broken heart. She writes in her recent letter, "I came to you after an alcoholic blackout and one visit to AA and told you the group talked about 'a Higher Power.' I didn't believe in God, but you said 'Imagine God exists, and see what happens.' On a parish retreat in Connecticut the next fall, I said yes to Jesus. Hallelujah! What a moment—and you led me with a gentle touch. So you are special to me for that and for much more—and I love you." Ruth has become a powerful and influential Christian, now serving on the board of one of our seminaries. As I look back, my words to her seem so ineffective and unimportant. It is a crisp reminder of how we must not underestimate the power of God to change human lives.

Last spring a middle-aged woman, Sarah, came to the church door as I was locking up after the last Sunday service. She said, "Dr. Colwell, you may not remember me, but I'm Sarah Goodwin, whom you refused to marry twenty-five years ago. I have a daughter twenty-three years old and finally got my courage up to leave my abusive husband, but I am tortured by this decision because I am now a Christian, and I believe that marriage is for keeps."

I remembered Sarah and Joe, her husband, having many conflicts between them and suggesting that they get some therapy and then consider marriage. He had stormed out in a rage, and they were married by a justice of the peace a few weeks later. Sarah sat in my office and told me how the advice that I had given them that day twenty-five years before had stuck in her mind. She said that I had been right in refusing to perform the marriage. I suggested to her that I didn't believe God desired for her to remain in a sick marriage. She had begged Joe for the two of them to get help, but he had thwarted each attempt. I told her that I had come to believe that divorce can be a sacrament instead of a sin. Her face brightened, and she began to reflect the grace of God that her soul had been seeking.

There have been times when I have written a sermon in five minutes, and it made a homerun, while most of the time I spend hours with few runs in the ballgame. There was one notable occasion when I quickly scratched off a prayer in a couple of minutes that, much to my surprise, traveled around the globe. Suzanne Massie, a parishioner and writer on Russian cultural life (*Land of the Firebird* and *Pavlovsk*), returned from her seventeenth trip to the Soviet Union in 1985 and shared with me her impression of the religious fervor and activity in Russia. She said that in that atheistic environment, more that sixty million Orthodox believers crowded churches each day. She told me that the people endured their suffering because of their deep faith. She empathized with their suffering because of a son, Robert Jr., born to her and her former husband, Robert K. Massie. Bobbie had been born with hemophilia. As she left Moscow, this time she asked a young woman friend, "What can I do for you?" The reply was, "Pray for us." Suzanne played the phrase over and over in her mind all the way back to New York. Soon after that, she came to my office to request that I write a prayer for the peoples of the Soviet Union that could be used in churches. Frankly, I forgot the request, but a couple of weeks later Suzanne called me at 10:00 PM and asked for the prayer. I promised to call back in fifteen minutes and quickly jotted down an eighteen-line prayer and dictated it to her over the phone. The prayer was subsequently picked up by *Guideposts* and became the cover story of its February 1985 issue. Norman Vincent Peale and the editors of *Guideposts* asked me to offer this prayer at the magazine's fortieth anniversary at the Waldorf Astoria so that its fifteen million readers around the country could recite it at the same time.

> Heavenly Father, Who holds and sustains all of creation with your love and whose hand is at work in all nations, we pray especially for the Russians and all other peoples of the Soviet Union, our brothers and sisters in their common pilgrimage. We thank you for their courage, their passion, vision and endurance. We pray for an outpouring of your spirit upon them, that faith may be strengthened, love made strong and hearts filled with your peace and promise. We ask that you protect, comfort and sustain all those who are suffering for you, and help them to know that they are not alone in their travail. And we pray that you will help us find ways to draw closer to each other and to you. We pray for these, your beloved people, for whom our Lord Jesus Christ gave His Life. Amen.

The prayer took flight and was passed from one denomination to another—to England, France and eastern Europe, beamed behind the Iron Curtain by the BBC and the Voice of America. In the end, many millions of people prayed the words of this quickly written, meager offering. The lesson seems to be, "Do your best because you never know who will read what you write or say!" It is amazing to me how the actions of God often move outward like rippling water. A tiny act can have enormous consequences when it becomes God's vehicle. The year before the prayer was written, Suzanne was called to advise President Ronald Reagan from 1984-1986 in his second term, meeting with him some twenty-two times to help him prepare for his successful meeting with Mikhail Gorbachev, the General Secretary of the Soviet Union. She called me before several visits to say, "The President wants me to come to the White House next week. Can we pray together?" Suzanne's influence on the president is not to be underestimated. I am humbled and amazed by the effect that our encounters often have on the larger world.

Divine Comedy

There is another important ingredient in ministry, and it's humor. God has equipped me with a number of gifts for ordained ministry, and one my favorites among these gifts, both effective and enjoyable, is humor. I get this from my mother who had a quick wit. I have come to believe that humor and laughter are sacramental and are to be found at the very heart of God. Laughter provides perspective and reduces stress. Richard Grein, former Episcopal Bishop of New York, once told a group of us clergy that "the Church is funny business, but we must take God seriously." A wise comment indeed! In parish ministry our funny bone is repeatedly tickled by an array of incidents that make a priest's life interesting as well as amusing. Church can be funny business.

The Alarming Ordination

My clergy assistant was to be ordained a priest at St. Barnabas in 1991. This ceremony usually took place at the Cathedral of St. John the Divine in New York but an exception was granted because he was a friend of Bishop Winterrowd of Colorado, who had also been a classmate of mine at General Seminary in the 1960s. The church was ready, and expectation and excitement filled the air. The long procession of the clergy and bishop lined up in a lounge near the church entrance. The thurible (incense pot) gave off great clouds of smoke as we proceeded solemnly into the church. Just as the bishop reached the steps of the crossing, the fire alarms and strobe lights all began their deafening symphony. The new fire alarm system had been installed the week before. No one knew how to turn it off, so the alarms continued as we raised our voices in competition with the strains of "God of the prophets, bless the prophets' heirs!" Our sound system director, Anne, went running to the parish hall basement to look on the control board for an "off" switch, which seemed to be amidst 150 other buttons and switches. The reader went to the lectern and read the words from Isaiah 6, "I saw the Lord sitting upon the throne, high and lifted up ... the house was filled with smoke and I said, 'Woe is me ...'" The congregation began to giggle and then to roar with laughter. Finally the alarm was turned off, only after the fire truck and twelve firemen arrived at the church door, ready for action. The smoking incense pot had been positioned directly under the smoke detector in the lounge just prior to the beginning of the service, and the smoke detector had been programmed to have a delayed response. This certainly was the most alarming ordination ever to take place in the Diocese of New York!

Who the Hell Are You?

In my first years at St. Barnabas, I went to visit a parishioner, the wife of Stan Getz, the late, great jazz saxophonist. Monica suggested that I wait for a few extra minutes before leaving so I could meet her husband, who was returning from the city. Finally I heard the screeching of brakes in the driveway and the screen door slamming closed. Stan went directly upstairs; his wife called him to come down. A few minutes later the Stan Getz I had heard so much about, dressed in a white terry cloth bathrobe, with hands on his hips, walked up to me, obviously a priest wearing a clerical collar, and said, "Who the hell are you?" I mumbled my name and parish connection and Stan retreated to better things. We later became friends and, even though he was Jewish, he came to church on a number of occasions, and I went on to bury one of his musical colleagues. "Who the hell are you?" The very question for any priest to have to answer. Probably *the* question of ordained ministry. Thank you, Stan.

Open Mike

Soon after St. Barnabas had a sound system installed, I was fitted with a microphone worn as a pendant around the neck before the late Sunday Eucharist began. Unaware of the "on" and "off" switches, I used the men's room a moment before the service. Later, I discovered that the entire congregation, waiting for the service to begin, heard me urinating and then heard the thunderous flush of the toilet. More incarnational theology and a huge dose of humility. Yes, even priests go to the bathroom, but not usually in church.

Funeral for a Ship

In the early 1970s, I received a phone call from a clergy friend who said that he was supposed to do a "funeral" service for the decommissioning of the HMS

Queen Mary at The Cunard Lines Pier on the Hudson River in Manhattan. His wife had been unexpectedly hospitalized, and he asked if I would take the service the next day; I agreed. Never having buried a great ship before, I used the Burial Office from The Book of Common Prayer. When I arrived at Pier 91 that Saturday noon, the breeze off the Hudson was very brisk. Most of the New York television and radio stations were present, as well as throngs of people. The English shiphands, whose lives and community had, for many decades, been centered on the Queen Mary, were pouring out of the bars on 12th Avenue, drunk and emotional. I was dressed in my white vestments; blown by the wind, they nearly sent me airborne. I began the service, "I am the resurrection and the life, says the Lord." I heard soft weeping that soon progressed to open sobbing and wailing. Grown men hugged each other and passed tissues.

I thought, "Good heavens, I never learned how to handle this in seminary!" The CEO and other Cunard Line authorities made speeches, and three wreaths for the departed were, with great solemnity, thrown off the pier into the Hudson River, only to be driven back under the dock by the wind.

"Out of the deep have I called unto thee, O Lord. Lord, hear my voice." The service was over. On the surface, even watching it on television later at home, it was a quirky, eccentric little event. Certainly professors of liturgics would find fault with an event that might have come across as the trivialization of religion. Yet, under it all, beneath the drunkenness and weeping, the wind and the misdirected memorial wreaths, the death of an important community was being acknowledged, and God was involved in this human moment. This was an instance when the church responded flexibly to a real need, albeit in a rather unscripted fashion—an early lesson in my priesthood that has often been repeated.

Humor in Scripture

Laughter is essential to life in the priesthood and in the Church. In the early church, the priest told jokes on the Sunday after Easter to ridicule the devil, who had been put in his place. It was called "Laughter Sunday." There are more than 250 biblical references to laughter. The Gospels are full of Jesus using humor, except we take these passages as serious and often miss the point.

- "It is easier for a camel to go through the eye of a needle than for the rich man to enter the Kingdom of God." (Mark 10:25) What a lasting image!

- "How many times should I forgive my brother?" Jesus answers "Seventy times seven." (Matthew 18:23-35) He certainly makes his point with exaggeration.
- "Why do you see the speck in your brother's eye and not the log in your own?" (Matthew 7:3) Ouch!
- "The tax collectors and whores go into the kingdom of God before you." (Matthew 21:31) Do I have your attention?
- "False prophets are dressed up in sheep's clothing, but they are really killer wolves. You will know them by their fruits." (Matthew 7:16) Sounds like Halloween.
- Jesus says to the crowds about to stone the woman taken in adultery, "Let him who is without sin cast the first stone." (John 8:7) Jesus pinches a raw nerve! Drop those stones you're hiding!
- The woman at the well says to Jesus, "I have been married before." Jesus says, "You tell the truth, woman, for you have been married five times and the one you are living with now is not your husband." The woman then says, "Sir, I perceive, you are a prophet!" (John 4:7-39) We used to laugh in seminary whenever this lesson was read.
- "Everyone who looks at a woman lustfully has already committed adultery with her in his heart. If your eye causes you to sin pluck it out and throw it away." (Matthew 5:27) Blindness, here we come!
- "Does anyone ever bring in a lamp and put it under a bowl or under a bed?" (Mark 4:21-22) Try that, and the house will burn down!

Jesus uses humor and exaggeration to express conflict in the human condition. The humor of Jesus is not a way of denying tears, but a way of affirming something deeper than tears. My friend, the late writer Madeleine L'Engle, once said, "Laughter saves us from falling all the way." Laughter is a rich gift that clergy and the religious enterprise need in order to keep perspective and to remain humble.

My wonderful secretary of twelve years, Sue Stanley, is of enormous help in using humor to soften the hard edges of parish ministry and in showing me how important it is to laugh at myself. She makes ordinary, tedious office work bright and fresh and helps us all as a staff to keep from "falling all the way." Her humor is infectious and makes our jobs a lot easier. Our daughter Susanna also has a keen sense of humor that brightens a room and draws people together.

Laughter is a great equalizer that cuts through class and status and can speak to almost everyone. We seem to be born with a common funny bone. Laughter has no boundary between the *religious* and the *secular*. The secular is usually seen as opposing the religious, but let's take a closer look. The collision of worlds here is both myth and heresy.

4

Embracing the Secular

o o o o o o o o o o o o o o o o o o o o o o o o o o o o o o
"… we have this treasure in earthen vessels.…"

—*2 Corinthians 4:7*

"There is nothing so secular that it cannot be sacred."

—*Madeleine L'Engle*

An Amphibious Calling

I sit in a Diocesan Council meeting, listening to boring committee reports, and begin to feel uneasy and impatient as several people speak. Their faith seems so easy, so well-programmed, so deficient in conflict and struggle; they utter such sweet phrases, such ecclesiastical platitudes.

"The Church is important."

"The diocese cares."

"The cathedral belongs to the people."

This meeting feels like a little enclave of spirituality, lofty and ever so pious and cut off from real life. I feel removed and different, not a good feeling. An unfiltered thought enters my head: I wonder about their private lives, their relationships, their addictions, their fears. What are they like when they hit the street? I wonder if they ever think about sex; somehow I doubt it. I feel hostile and impatient. Somehow I want to feel less religious. What I hear in this meeting is not what I feel in my bones.

Once the meeting is over, I grab my coat and quickly leave, walking in the shadow of the great Cathedral of St. John the Divine, huge, cold, and grey. I walk west on 111th Street. There is a boy trying unsuccessfully to train his Doberman to heel and sit. An ambulance races up Broadway toward St. Luke's Hospital.

Turning right onto Broadway, I encounter a crazed, tattered man who invites me to join him in singing "Yankee Doodle." I try to hide my embarrassment and hurry on. A passing Columbia student says to his friend, "They don't understand the socialist cause, those Bush bastards!" At 115th Street a perfumed prostitute slips into a bar. Two young men are making a drug transaction only a few feet from a police car. A little boy grabs an apple from an outside fruit stand and disappears onto a side street. I pass a cafeteria and see everyone lined up at the counter and staring straight ahead at the wall, each in his own world. I feel lonely and cold. Suddenly a giant chocolate cruller in a doughnut shop window beckons me, and I thumb my nose at Weight Watchers; as I munch on it, I feel a little brighter.

Here is real life with all its frustrated and broken dreams. Real people. No platitudes. Despair, hope, life—all mixed up together. I begin to feel at home here on the street, surrounded by many fringe people, amid the semi-OK—those who taste dried crusts of bread, believing them to be the best they can have. Here, life is lived in painful truth, and illusion is often traded for what cannot be faced. Here on the street, I choose to cast my lot, not in the antiseptic ivory towers of neatly ordered spiritual abstraction.

A shoeshine and a visit to a bookstore later, my head still swirling, I walk east on 112th Street toward the great monument to religion. I feel drawn to enter the Cathedral where I was ordained a priest many years before. The battle lines seem drawn. Why do I feel that the street and the House of God are colliding? I hear a tour guide mechanically describing the Cathedral's proportions, concluding with an outright lie: "The acoustics here are superb." Is this the street or the Church? What strange feelings are mine. Am I a man without a country? An ordained priest welcomed by the streets and uncomfortable in the Church? The street feels more real and less pretentious than the Church. This realization is uncomfortable.

I hear the beautiful, recorded choir of King's College, Cambridge coming from the gift shop. Their voices reverberate off the great vaulted arches and the thick gray granite walls. Heavenly, peaceful voices form a synthesis, a unity, hinting at resolution. I hear a whisper deep within my heart—"There is no battle here between earth and heaven." I suddenly realize that I am an amphibious creature with one foot in the street and the other in the Church. The street is like a lovely ocean where we play with the surf and the wind, and the church is dry land where we look for safety and solid footing. It would be far easier to plant both feet firmly in either world. Some choose to stay within the safety of the Church, to keep primarily Christian friends, to adopt a Christian vocabulary, and to work hard at being *spiritual*. On the other hand, for many, the streets hold a great attraction. They speak of pleasure, of wealth, of success, all of which seem so concrete and attainable. I pause at the nativity window and realize that mine is an amphibious calling; that's what the Christmas story is all about—*And the word became flesh and dwelt among us.* Earth becomes the womb of heaven so that God may be born in the manger of human experience.

There is a profound link between the street and the Church, between earth and heaven. Our spirituality must be anchored in the earth and our flesh must see the glory of God. John Keble, the Oxford cleric, wrote of this in the mid 1800s, "Two worlds are ours: 'tis only sin forbids us to decry, the mystic heaven and earth within, plain as the sea and sky." Heaven and earth need not collide; in God's plan, they are inexorably connected.

All of Me

One of the funniest and best metaphors for our divided selves was brilliantly portrayed in the 1984 film *All of Me,* starring Steve Martin and Lily Tomlin. Tomlin is a wealthy heiress who dies and is cremated. An urn carrying her ashes falls from a window, hitting Steve Martin on the head and causing Tomlin's soul to pass into half of his body. Martin spends the remainder of the film as a divided creature, half himself and half someone else. One of the most hilarious scenes shows Martin walking down the sidewalk, half strutting and half slinking, and later standing in front of a men's room urinal, his body at war with itself. Many of us Christians live as if we were two persons in one body. We try desperately to keep the spiritual and the physical separate, much to our detriment. Alan Jones, Dean of Grace Cathedral in San Francisco, says that "spirituality is the art of making connections between what is around us and God."[1] Our work as Christians is to heal the split we have inherited.

The Religious Relative

I have a relative who became a "Christian" in the late 70s—which has become a curse for the rest of my family. Sharon began identifying what was of God and what was of the devil. This was quite a shock to her Episcopal family. Suddenly dancing, card playing, movies, and Christmas trees were off limits. She took me aside at a family party to inform me that "the Episcopal Church is possessed by the devil." I thanked her for the information and suggested that the best way to fight the devil is to stay close to Christ. She was not convinced. Sharon has done considerable damage to our family throughout the years. She puts us on hate-filled mailing lists and sends us articles warning us of governmental involvement in a conspiracy to use our Social Security numbers in order to establish a world government led by the United Nations. The plot, she insists, is to destroy God's true word and to establish satanic rule in the world. She is a very persistent evangelist whose delusion is based on the split between religious and secular, spirit and flesh, the devil's greatest weapon. We have seen televangelists who live on two separate tracks: public piety, private promiscuity. St. Teresa of Avila warned us of this possibility, commenting, "God deliver me from people so spiritual that they want to turn everything into perfect contemplation no matter what!" Flesh and spirit, the secular and the religious, cannot be separated; all are bound together by a God who enters creation and human flesh.

Collision on the Dock

I grew up on an island off the coast off Maine, in a family with a long involvement in the lobster trade. My great-great-grandfather built the first lobster pound (an enclosed cove) in the United States. My father, uncles, and cousin were wholesale lobster dealers who ran businesses in Stonington and Boothbay Harbor. My cousin Dick and I worked for many summers on the docks, buying lobsters from fishermen, unloading fish from the holds of herring boats, shoveling bait, and loading trucks for transport to Boston. This was an earthy environment where sexual jokes and physical bravado ruled. I will always be grateful for this education because it anchored me in the earth and served as a counterweight to my inherent "spiritual" side, which I clearly inherited from my mother. I remember the Methodist minister from our local church coming to the dock one day to get lobsters for his guests. The word was quickly passed to "clean up your language" and to toss in a few attempted "religious" references.

"Reverend Lacy," asked Clyde, "How is the God business going?" Snickers could be heard from Earl, who almost choked on his cigar.

"A lot of souls need saving around here," said Morris, a smirk on his face. When the minister left the dock, there was a sense of relief from the tension-charged air. Phew! Things could now return to normal, i.e., keeping secular and religious divorced from each other.

Hide the Cocktail

One day, shortly after the incident on the dock, Mr. Lacy came to pay a pastoral visit to my parents in their home. It was about 6:00 PM, and my father had just made cocktails for my mother and himself. They began to enjoy their drinks when the doorbell rang. When realizing who the visitor was, my mother sharply ordered my father, "Albert, pour the drinks down the drain and spray the kitchen before you let John in." I remember thinking, even then, what a waste of liquor this was. The irony of this scene was soon to be realized when my parents discovered that Mr. Lacy was known to enjoy a cocktail himself from time to time.

"There's a Priest in the House"

Shortly after I was ordained a priest, I went to a party given by my fiancée and her two apartment mates on Riverside Drive near Columbia University. The guests were from different walks of life. There was Ron, a black psychiatrist, and Kenny a gay decorator, both tenants in the building; there were many guests from the field of social work, some students, some professors, two friends who worked for an anti-poverty program in Harlem, a couple of young lawyers, and several Wall Street traders. This group of some twenty-five people made their own drinks at the kitchen bar. I was not wearing a clerical collar.

While mixing a drink, a young social worker said to me, "We'd better be careful because I understand there's a priest here tonight."

I responded "It's no fun if we have to be careful!"

About forty-five minutes later, after I had been identified, I watched several guests whisper to each other as I approached. I felt like another species! I suspect that they were playing back the tape of their conversations with me through their own "religious" filters.

Despite what we are taught, we human beings inhabit only one world, only one seamless reality. There is no division between secular and religious. It is essential to remove the wall that designates a church building as holy and the local bar as secular. There is no sense in which a Christian has to turn away from the world in order to meet God. The tension we feel between the world of the spirit and the world of the flesh is not a boundary between two worlds but the meeting point for two parts of one reality.

"You Can't Lie"

My oldest daughter came home from school, very upset, one day when she was in the first grade. Her friend Marny had said to her, "Emily, you can't lie because your father is a priest."

Emily thought for a few seconds and responded, "What does your father do?"

"He's a doctor."

Emily, with a giant counter-punch, replied, "Then you can't get sick!"

We rob ourselves when we lock people into their roles and require that they act according to perceived stereotypes. I, for one, am insulted when someone pegs me as a clergyman and thrilled when I'm told "I had no idea" because I often find that the stereotypes are insulting and shallow and that they trivialize my role. Stereotyping is a dangerous sport and allows us to lock a person into a role that makes us feel comfortable and safe from any confrontation with the unknown in that other person.

Our Humbling Children

Having young children makes it difficult for parents to maintain an illusion of a perfect, well-mannered, civilized family. Our children are preoccupied with their bodily functions, ask embarrassing questions at the wrong time, and sometimes run naked through the living room during a dinner party. Children leave no room for us to pretend we are not close to the earth. How easy it is to write about family life while avoiding really living it; to talk about Christianity while hiding from the world. There is no honest way of remaining aloof, untainted. Children force us to keep our spirituality anchored in the earth. After all, that's what Jesus did.

Laughing Jesus

I have a poster, "Laughing Jesus," hanging on my office wall. I remember a visiting nun moving closer to the picture to study it only to discover, to her horror, in the fine print at the bottom, the copyright name, *Playboy* magazine. In most circles Jesus is associated as a spiritual, feet-slightly-off-the-ground religious figure. The poster speaks fondly of the human Jesus, who is depicted with a full belly laugh—a Jesus who is also fully a man, who gets hungry and thirsty, who goes to the bathroom, who is sad at the death of Lazarus, and who gets angry at the money-changers in the temple. This portrait anchors divinity in human flesh and motivates us to integrate both flesh and spirit. The poster serves as a kind of Rorschach test that instantly tells me, by a person's reaction, how healthy his understanding of God is. We Christians have done a lot of damage by pitting flesh against spirit, secular against religious, making sex shameful and physical enjoyment of creation a perversion. Because of this damage, for many people, Christianity has become toxic instead of liberating and integrative.

The Ordinary

My spiritual director and friend, author Barbara Crafton, has the uncommon ability to see the extraordinary within the ordinary, to see God in the common. Her approach to life is profoundly incarnational. My own ministry is full of God showing up in places other than the conventionally religious or the expected. I am aware of the presence of God in the breaking waves of the Atlantic Ocean at Fire Island, at the magnificence of a summer sunset, in the midst of a pastoral counseling session with a woman who is deciding to leave her abusive husband, at the birth of our children, in lovemaking, in the taste of chocolate, in swimming, in listening to Mendelssohn, and in the words "I love you." Elizabeth Barrett Browning captured this sense of God in the ordinary in her poem *Aurora Leigh*.

> "Earth's crammed with heaven,
> And every common bush afire with God;
> But only he who sees takes off his shoes;
> The rest sit round it and pluck blackberries."

Faith and the Work Place

One of the most challenging areas for a priest in parish ministry is in helping parishioners make connections between their employment and their faith. Increasingly, people speak of their dog-eat-dog work environments on the one hand and their Christianity and church involvement on the other. Often, there seems to be a great gulf fixed between the two. Church and Christian values are easily applied to the family, but the workplace is seen as a pagan, capitalistic environment that doesn't lend itself to religion. William F. Bellais, an Episcopal priest, speaks of this issue. "The church's failure to understand the sanctity of secular work has fostered a culture in which religion and work are separate departments."[2] Rarely do I see a parishioner who genuinely loves her work and is filled with passion and purpose in connection with that work. Work becomes, rather, a means to an end, a way of providing for ourselves and our families. I am fully aware of how blessed I am to be doing what I love, what I do best, and what provides meaning and engagement for my life. I believe that if the ordained ministry didn't exist, I would have had to create it. My gifts and the needs of parish life are a wonderful fit. Many people fear that if they were to seriously apply their faith in the workplace, there would be a clash of cultures. We are working hard in my parish to help people make such a connection between work and faith. Piety will not cut it in the workplace, and neither will religious language. What does impress others however, is an integrated, whole person who speaks and acts out of core values. The current image of Christian evangelists proselytizing in the workplace should make us all shudder. Such activity gives God a bad name and makes Christianity appear as a trite extra tacked onto our lives.

The Goodness of Creation

Underlying all we believe and do as Christians is an understanding that creation is fundamentally good. In the Biblical account in Genesis, in the beginning, after each day of creation, God reviews what he has accomplished and declares that "it is good." At the end of creation, God goes so far as to declare that "it is *very* good." Creation remains fundamentally good, even though tainted by evil and sin. This concept is reinforced by God entering human flesh in Jesus of Nazareth, loving creation from within, slowly drawing everything, including evil and death, into that victorious love. Christianity, thus, profoundly affirms all creation, including flesh and the whole material universe.

As Christians and as human beings, we need to reclaim the goodness and unity of all of creation, of flesh and of spirit. This is really the best of news in a world that has lost any sense of a unified reality. Wherever we find the splits in our behavior, God is calling us to bring the pieces together. This is the deeper meaning of salvation: to make whole, to make healthy, to integrate. This view affords no room for dualism because God has brought all together and shown us, in Jesus, what it looks like to be saved.

There is a powerful story in Acts 10:9-16 about St. Peter's vision. He was very hungry one day and wanted to eat. While dinner was being prepared, he fell into a trance and saw the heavens opened and a great sheet being lowered to the earth; on it were all kinds of animals, reptiles, and birds. A voice said, "Peter, kill and eat." But Peter said, "No, Lord, I have never eaten anything that is common or unclean." And God said, "What I have cleansed, you must not call common." Our job is to embrace life and the material world, to see God in all things. Worlds do not collide in this view because it is God's world and it has been declared good.

Secularization as Gift

The Church often decries the secularization of society and sees it as an attack on religion; in doing so, the Church misses a golden opportunity. I often read in church periodicals that the church is being overlooked by society, that the respect once enjoyed is missing, that atheists are out to get us and that the secularization of the western world is killing religion. Secularization is good for Christianity and for the Church because it forces us to find new ways to engage with real life and with those who know little of the church or with those who have been badly disillusioned by it. This secularization is at once both judgment and opportunity. I believe God is calling the Church back into the secular sphere, this world where we live. The Church is being called to move beyond its cozy, churchy, pious positions to engage with real issues and real life. The Church must embrace this important journey. Our age and its skepticism and discomfort in regard to organized religion and dogma are all gifts to the Church. We can go on using our religious language and demanding allegiance to *right belief*, or we can find the old truths in current cultural patterns and experiences and help people discover the Gospel in the midst of their own lives. Theologian Karl Rahner points this out. "The theological problem today is to find the art of drawing religion out of man, not pumping it into him. The redemption has happened. The Holy Spirit is in man. The art is to help men become what they are."[3]

May the Church stop attacking the secular and begin recognizing it as God's vehicle for shaking up the church and reaching people in our generation! Our task is to embrace the secular—indeed, all of life—with courage and purpose because it is the place where God shows up even amidst conflict, doubt, and dragons. Underlying the world we live in, however, is the truth of God's amazing grace, which is radical and rather un-American. However, that grace provides the safety net for us to experience acceptance and support on our journey.

5

Radical Grace

> *"... There is nothing you can do to make God love you less—absolutely nothing, for God already loves you and will love you forever."*
>
> —Desmond Tutu

The Outrageous Paradox

I have never started a new day by saying to myself, "I'm going to do some growing today." That's just not the way I am built. If the truth be known, I don't grow unless I'm under pressure to do so, unless I'm cornered, and there is no escape! Growth for me happens when I get hit over the head with a club. Addiction, depression, surgery, financial difficulty, or the threat of losing an important relationship—now, these get my attention!

One of the most important passages in the New Testament is found in St. Paul's second letter to the Corinthian Church, 2 Corinthians 12:2-10.

> "And to keep me from being too self-assured a thorn was given to me in my flesh to harass me and keep me from being too elated. Three times I besought the Lord about this that it should leave me; but he said to me, 'My grace is sufficient for you, for my power is made perfect in your weakness.' I will all the more gladly boast of my weaknesses, that the power of Christ may rest upon me ... for when I am weak, then I am strong."

We don't really know what Paul's "thorn" was, although conjecture has covered the gamut from epilepsy to an injured foot to bad eyesight to being gay. Whatever his issue was, his prayers were not answered the way he desired. He discovered the central gospel truth that God's power is made perfect in weakness. *Power in weakness.* This motto should be above the entrance to every parish church, every cathedral—yes, above every one's home and desk. To the world at large, this paradox makes no sense. In fact, to most Christians and to many clergy, it makes no sense either. It isn't what we want to hear; the human and corporate focus is on power and strength.

The "Big Mouth from the South," Ted Turner, said a few years ago that "Christianity is for losers." He has subsequently retracted this statement, and his ex-wife, Jane Fonda, became a Christian, which seemingly helped lead to their divorce. Turner, however, was not far off the mark; Christianity does see power in losing in opposition to playing the winning game.

So, how does "power in weakness" work? The secret, I believe, has to do with God getting our attention, or for us to stop long enough for God to be able to get our attention. This certainly happened with 9/11. I was interviewed for a book and DVD shortly after the tragedy. The book has a marvelous title, *Will the Dust Praise You?* It is filled with stories of people turning to God in the midst of this tragedy, of communities being formed out of people's sense of weakness, fear, and suffering. History is rich with great figures whose weaknesses became the vehicles for witness to God's power and Love: Martin Luther King, Mohandas Gandhi, Dietrich Bonhoeffer.

There's an old saying, "Man's extremity is God's opportunity." Each of us have our own personal trials and limits, our personal thorn in our flesh. Our job is to identify these places where we have no control of the way something will turn out or that area where our lives are unmanageable. These can become the places where God's grace can be discovered. In these dark places, God is waiting to shed light. Peter Gomes, Professor of Christian Morals at Harvard, says, "Faith is not some abstract theological construct confined to an ancient formulary of the Christian faith."[1] It is in weakness that the God of grace can powerfully enter our lives and begin to transform them inch by inch. I find funerals are important times, when people are accessible due to pain and loss, to understand such a paradox. Hurt and heartache allow the message to be heard, often for the first time.

"Turning Our Wills and Lives Over"

I can be a very willful person, stubborn and set in my opinions. I sometimes think I inherited these genes from my Germanic ancestry on my mother's side. I am a New Englander, raised with a good dose of stoicism, where overwork was considered a great virtue. "God helps those who help themselves" was posted under the sign that read "Welcome to Maine." Self-determination was an important characteristic; willpower was of the essence. I think impatience is a trait of willful people. I hate to wait for traffic lights to turn green and get hostile in traffic jams and in long checkout lines at the supermarket. I am the kind of person who begins the day with a long list of the things I need to accomplish in the order of their importance. I become tense and irritated when my plans are interrupted, which they usually are. I served on our local volunteer ambulance corps for seven years and would be on duty for a twenty-four-hour shift, accompanied by the ever-present beeper. Whenever I was involved in a good television program or engaged in an engrossing conversation and the beeper would buzz, I would feel annoyed at the interruption. I am goal-oriented, often sacrificing relationships on the altar of goal accomplishment. Control seems to be characteristic of willful people; believing that they can be in charge of everything.

Alcoholics Anonymous taught me one of the most important lessons of my life. The first step of the program says "We admitted we were powerless ... and that our lives had become unmanageable." By the time I discovered AA, I was more than ready to admit that applying willpower to deal with my life had not worked. Powerlessness, a concept I had always hated, now began to appeal to me. The third step of AA says, "Made a decision to turn our wills and our lives over to the care of God." I had been able to exercise enormous willpower in my life; the problem was that it had not worked. I was not up to the task of managing my life! God began showing me that turning my will and my life over to him actually worked. So I began in 1986 to practice God-power instead of willpower and discovered that it was effective. I have found myself less impatient, less angry, and less eager to take on another person's problem if it isn't my responsibility. The simple act of turning my will over to God is liberating. The Serenity Prayer, written by Richard Niehbuhr and abbreviated by AA, has become a marvelous mantra for sorting out where my responsibility stops and God's begins.

"God grant me the serenity to accept the things I cannot change—the courage to change the things I can, and the wisdom to know the difference." In return, I feel the presence of God often tangibly surrounding me. I have learned that I don't have to be perfect. (I was the only one who labored under that illusion.) I realize that when I make mistakes and admit them, I can make amends and move on. It is a great relief to give up being a demanding perfectionist with myself and others.

Much to my dismay, I have come to realize that there is often more honest faith in God practiced in the parish halls and church basements where twelve-step programs are often held than in the worship space in the churches themselves. In a strange but marvelous way, I have discovered God anew in the secular halls of AA. They are, in fact, hallowed by God's presence. I only wish that the Church could discover this. My self-will kept God at a distance until I entered AA at the age of forty-nine. I had been perplexed by the idea of surrender until I reached a dead-end road and was willing to try another approach out of desperation. I have come to know that control and willpower do not lead to joy and freedom. Allowing God to be in the driver's seat became a lot easier after I came to realize that I hadn't done such a great job so far in my life. In my early days in AA, I was afraid to let go for fear of losing my independence and of becoming a weak, dependent creature. The truth I have discovered is a paradox: the more I am willing to depend on God, the more authentic I become, and the calmer and more accepting of outcomes I can be. Dependence on God is actually a means of becoming truly free.

It Is Not About Goodness

A parishioner said to me the other day, "I'm not sure whether I'm going to end up in heaven or hell." It was an innocent comment. Underlying her words was an assumption about the amount of goodness she possessed. I have a sign in my office that is really a diagnostic question. It reads, "How much sin can I get away with and still go to heaven?" Will I be moral enough, in the end, to get there?

I remember, particularly as a teenager, worrying that I wouldn't be good enough to squeeze through the pearly gates. I remember hearing the minister of the Stonington Methodist Church speak about grace as a free gift of God but then spend most of the sermon demanding righteousness. Somehow I knew that the gate was too high and that I would never be able to get through. Occasionally I will listen to the radio or television early on Sunday mornings while getting ready for my first service. So many of the preachers talk about grace and God's love but preach law and requirement; Often there seems to be a serious disconnect. How is it that such wonderful news suddenly turns, like a curve ball, into bad news?

There's an old southern saying, "Y'all be good now." Somehow that message seems to have infected our Sunday schools like a bad virus. Alec Vidler, the British theologian, after a lengthy visit to the United States, reported back home that the message of the American pulpit seemed to be, "Let me suggest that you try to be good." I have come to believe that the heart of the Christian Gospel is not primarily about being good but rather about our dependence on God's grace and of God's acceptance of us. It is in the life, passion, and resurrection of Jesus that we see what God's love looks like. In Jesus we see God's love absorbing the evil and perversity of human nature and offering to change us. If we depend on our own goodness to make it into heaven, may God help us all!

"Amazing grace! How sweet the sound,
That saved a wretch like me!
I once was lost but now am found,
Was blind but now I see."

Our primary task is to accept the fact of God's acceptance that Easter reveals to us. Too good to be true? You bet it is! The Church often distorts this message by using rules as its standard of measurement for salvation-success. This is depressing news. The church too often sells goodness as the goal. In fact, the unconditional love of God, is an amazingly radical concept. Nothing, absolutely nothing, is required of us to be loved fully and completely by God. Our good works become a response to unconditional acceptance. The Christian message that we read in Ephesians 2:8-9 has been all but obscured:

"For by grace you have been saved through faith; and this is not your own doing; it is the gift of God—not because of works, lest anyone should boast."

The Christian way of life results from the coming together of our weakness with the love of God. Many of us Christians are exhausting ourselves trying to be good enough, to collect enough chits to cash in on the day of judgment. We are much like Alice in *Through the Looking Glass*, running feverishly in order to stay in the same place. We, on the other hand, have to learn to stand still in order to get somewhere. Repentance actually means turning around and getting back on the right road. We need to reach out and join hands with the one who has already arrived and who can love us into the kingdom. Recognizing our need for God is the beginning of this process. The writer and priest Robert Capon says: "If only they could see that Christianity starts by telling you that you have no place left to go because you're already home free, and no favor to earn because God sees you in his beloved Son and thinks you're the greatest thing since sliced bread. All you have to do is explore the crazy Mystery of your acceptance. Why do they always want to do it the hard way?"[2]

The beginning point for hearing the good news is our sense of being lost, our desperate need. In a real sense, we cannot even repent without first being moved by God's grace. God is the one who sends out a rescue party, finds us, and then declares that we're home free. Repentance doesn't save a lost soul. The soul, upon experiencing acceptance, can be motivated to repent and begin to change. We are loved into repentance. It's all about the love of God. The universe is about this love. Human existence is supposed to be about this love. Even in death, love is exposed. God's love permeates every leafy cell, every child, every furry creature, every scaly fish of the sea, every cloud, and the heart of every person. Yet evil is at war with love. Easter tells us that love has won. That it is the stronger power. Yes, it's all about love, so good news abounds! My current clergy assistant, Joel Daniels, preached one of the best sermons on grace that I ever hope to hear. He said, "This grace is hard to take, hard to look at straight on, so we have to go through images; look at Jesus on the cross and see God there and realize—Wow, there is nothing I can do to make God love me less—absolutely nothing. And that goes for me, and for all the other billions of people in the world."[3]

Aggie

I will never forget a stranger who paid an unexpected visit one rainy summer afternoon and showed me what God's grace looks like.

It was a humid, mid-August day, and the rain was coming down in sheets; the heavens were filled with thunder and streaks of lightning. A young woman, perhaps in her early thirties, appeared at the back door of the rectory with a big black garbage bag slung over her shoulder containing all of her worldly possessions. I sat on the porch, gave her a sandwich and something to drink, and we talked. "I'm Aggie, and I'm working my way up from the City (New York) to the Catskills to try to find work in one of the summer hotels." As we talked, I realized that there was something different about Aggie. She gave me no sob story but was disarmingly open, honest, and filled with gratitude. "I can't begin to tell you," she said, "how good God has been to me. He always gives me exactly what I need when I need it. I am truly blessed." Aggie belonged to no church and never had, but she knew God in a way that many Christians have never grasped. Her gratitude overflowed to make her a powerful secular evangelist. As she broke bread, I sensed Jesus was with us. As the Gospel tells us, "He was known to them in the breaking of the bread." Yes, Jesus himself sat there, made visible through Aggie's gratitude and grace. I gave her money to take the train upstate and drove her to the station. That visit is indelibly etched on my mind and heart. Aggie really understood grace. As Brother David Stiendl-Rast says, "Even the predictable turns into surprise the moment we stop taking it for granted."[4]

God's grace is about radical hospitality. It is about being welcomed and accepted as special and valued.

Radical Hospitality

In 1996 Judy and I led a group of twenty-two people on a tour of Greece and Turkey. We spent one night in the western Turkish city of Izmir (ancient Smyrna) on the Aegean coast. We arrived in the late afternoon after a long bus ride from Troy. After a banquet provided by the hotel, five of us decided we needed to get some exercise and fresh air. After a long stroll in Konak Square, we decided to find a coffee shop and enjoy some local color. We discovered many bakery and sweet shops but none serving coffee or tea. Starbucks had not yet arrived in Izmir! In one shop we tried to ask the shopkeepers in English where we could find coffee and tea, but they didn't understand. Suddenly a man off the street approached us and asked in broken English what we were looking for. He told us to be seated and to wait for a few minutes and that he would return. We waited and waited and played guessing games as to where he had gone and if he would return. About forty-five minutes later, the man entered the shop carrying a large silver tray replete with silver-handled glasses of coffee and tea, a sugar bowl, and a pitcher of milk.

"This is for you," he said, "Welcome to Izmir." He had gone up the street to his apartment and made the refreshments for us. As he sat and talked with us about American movies he had seen, I asked him how he had learned English.

"From CNN," he replied. He went on to tell us that showing hospitality to strangers is essential for Turks. He said, "Anyone who comes to our door must be treated as a guest of Allah." That experience became deeply rooted in our hearts as we left Izmir the next morning. This had been a wonderful example of radical hospitality which Jesus, also a Middle Easterner, often pointed to.

Jesus and Hospitality

On one occasion, Jesus provided five loaves of bread and two fish and fed five thousand people on the hillside of Capernaum overlooking the Sea of Galilee. And, at the end of the story, there were twelve baskets of food left over (Mark 6:37-44). God's grace is plentiful and provides more than we need; it is in God's nature to do so. We see this again in Jesus' parable of radical grace in the story of the lost son. The father had two sons. The younger asked for his inheritance and left the family, while the older son remained at home and was responsible and faithful. The younger son went far away, squandered his possessions, and lived a wild, irresponsible lifestyle. Eventually he fell on difficult times and ended up feeding pigs, the worst job for a good Jew. He was desperate and hungry, with no options left, so he decided to return to his father and offer to work as a day laborer. His father saw him coming and with compassion ran to meet him and kissed him. The son said, "Father, I have sinned against God and you and am no longer worthy to be called your son." But his father asked his servants to bring the best robe, a special ring for his finger, and shoes for his feet, and to make a feast and to celebrate his son's return. The older brother was angry that he had remained faithful and hadn't received such lavish recognition, but his father said,

"It is fitting to make merry and be glad, for this your brother was dead, and is alive; he was lost, and is found" (Luke 15:11-32). God is like this, Jesus tells his disciples; his door is always open, his arms extended in invitation. Does God require right behavior for acceptance? The unbelievable answer appears to be "No." God, however, is always calling us to come home and to embrace the fact we are fully, unconditionally accepted. This is radical grace and is the most difficult Christian belief to swallow even for the church, but it's the gospel. Paul Zahl, priest and author, calls the church to task for its difficulty with grace. "In almost every moment of historical time, the church has come down on grace. It has been fearful of it, competitive with it, and hostile to it. Church is typically the enemy of grace." [5]

The Magic Eyeglasses

I have a new pair of eyeglasses. If you must know, they are trifocals. Yes, I'm of that vintage. These lenses cost me a fortune; it probably would have made more monetary sense to get new eyes. Anyway, one of the "special" items I paid extra for was a hard coating sprayed on the lenses at the factory that makes them repel dirt and grime. I rarely need to wash the lenses with soap and water; a simple wipe does the trick.

When I occasionally get a spot of grease on the one lens, I become obsessed with seeing only the dirty spot and not looking through it to what is beyond. I think there is a spiritual parallel here; perhaps that of seeing beyond our imperfections and sins to a larger perspective: the love and grace that God is waiting to share with us. When I see through and beyond the dirty spots on my lenses, I am aware of the giant holly tree filled with red-breasted robins just outside of my office window. At least a hundred of them, and in mid-February! Beyond the robins I see a row of tall, lacy trees that run along the Croton Aqueduct, which is at the backside of the church property. Looking further through these magnificent trees, I can see the sparkling waters of the Hudson River. My soul begins to soar as I move beyond my myopic prison and begin to see a richer, more open, expansive world that provides perspective for the rest of my life. I have a sense of well-being, of nurture and safety and of God's involvement in his creation. Life seems wondrous.

This expensive pair of glasses helps me understand that God is calling me to see beyond my spots and imperfections to a world of grace and gift, a world that puts my sins in perspective. This new view draws me into a relationship with God that begins to change my paradigm and my understanding of life and the future.

I do thank God that I paid an extra hundred dollars to get my lenses sprayed with magic liquid. It helps me to see beyond the spots.

The concept of God's radical grace also requires us to challenge our myopic, self-centered views of those we perceive as "other." There are countless other fellow human beings whom God loves and who are in a relationship with God. It is an important part of our growth to be in dialogue with those of other faiths. Grace extends the invitation and is waiting to greet us on the other side of the fence.

6

Neither Jew nor Greek: Interfaith Dialogue

o o o o o o o o o o o o o o o o o o o o o o o o o o o o o
"There is neither Jew nor Greek, there is neither slave nor free, there is neither male nor female; for you are all one in Christ Jesus."

—*Galatians 3:28*

"The god of exclusivism is an idol."

—*Michael Ingham*

Exclusivity

I recently heard of an Episcopal priest who sent out a letter to newcomers in his parish, a letter that certainly clarified where he stood theologically. In his letter he said that Ted Bundy, the serial killer who had become a Christian before his execution, was in heaven, but that Gandhi, the Indian leader who didn't become a Christian, was now in hell. Sir Arnold Toynbee, the great historian would call this "the plague of exclusivity."

Three months before 9/11, I attended a meeting of Muslims at the Interfaith Center of New York and heard that a small group of Muslims had given a donation to Senator Hillary Clinton's senatorial campaign. Because of this action, they were immediately associated by conservative Christian critics with those who had bombed the U.S.S. Cole. The entire Islamic community was deeply hurt by this irrational and hysterical association.

St. Paul, writing to the Church in Galatia, tells the Christians that when they are baptized and are associated with Jesus, all distinctions are broken down. I have come to believe that Jesus reveals a truth about God's love to the whole human race, not restricted to Christians, because he came for the whole world.

A Vision

A few years ago Judy and I sailed into Istanbul at Sunset. The tall minarets stood against the red sky. We sailed past the Golden Horn, where Hagia Sophia, the Blue Mosque, and the Topkapi Museum are located. This city of twelve million, one of the most beautiful cities of the world, holds a rich history as well as tall, modern skyscrapers in its embrace. This Muslim city is located half in Europe and half in Asia.

The day after we arrived, while looking out over the Bosphorus, I experienced a powerful vision that all people are one. All of humanity is linked together by the God who made us and continues to breathe life into our various tribes. We are inextricably connected to others who are different from ourselves; we are one family of God on this planet.

The Human Genome Project reported that all people are essentially the same, regardless of race. Andy Grove, the CEO of Intel, said in an interview that the world is becoming a global community in culture, business, and communication, and that this is changing the way we relate to each other.

Who Is In and Who Is Out?

St. Augustine once said that "God has many people whom the Church does not." What is it about some Christians who resent grace being given to non-Christians? Those who have to "Christianize" things and people before they will have anything to do with them? Those who listen only to Christian music, go to Christian schools, use Christian plumbers or electricians? Jesus always hung out with sinners and those outside of the accepted establishment. We are told by Jesus that we are all accepted as children of God. In fact, we need each other in this life in order to make it through, and increasingly we will need to cooperate with the rest of the world if we are to survive. Someone has said that the gate to heaven is so low that no one can enter it except on his or her knees—and everyone, black, white, Asian, gay, straight, rich, poor, Christian, Muslim, Jew, Buddhist, Hindu, or atheist, will have to go through that gate. It is also said that the doorway is so low and narrow that it will take others' hands to pull us through. Will we turn down willing hands because the person offering to help us is different or doesn't meet our criteria for a correct, beautiful, and human perfect specimen? I doubt it very much. I believe that accepting others is always tied to first accepting ourselves. Where there is prejudice in us, there is discomfort about something in us, a fear of some defect. In God's kingdom, however, an acceptance and openness to those who are different from us expands our vision and opens us up to the gifts we need. Others complete something missing in us; God made the world this way, and it is not a mistake.

A famous hymn reinforces St. Paul's words to the Galatians. "In Christ there is no east or west, in him no north or south, but one great fellowship of love throughout the whole wide world." The family of Jesus is a new concept! Our likes and dislikes are not what bring us together. It is rather in Christ that we catch a vision of inclusion. He is the one who "breaks down the dividing wall of hostility" as the writer of Hebrews puts it. As we mingle with "the other" and find our common humanity, we get a clearer picture of God and of ourselves. We are not complete in isolation. We cannot accept others until we first accept ourselves. Alan Jones says it well. "When we begin to accept our inner plurality, we get less frightened of others who manifest a different tribal mix."[1]

An Open Parish

When I had my vision in Istanbul, I had already been a priest for thirty-eight years and rector of the Church of St. Barnabas for twenty-nine. Throughout my years at St. Barnabas, I had begun recognizing the thin line that existed between "believers," "non-believers" and the host of others who were at different points on the continuum of faith. I have come to understand all human beings as pilgrims on a journey, some remarkably articulate and others stumbling along, doing their best to make some sense out of their lives and experiences. The idea of forcing everyone to embrace the core truths of Christianity in order to be saved or to belong rightfully to a Christian community began to make me feel uncomfortable. I am not suggesting that there are no core truths, but I am suggesting that the clergy's job is to meet people where they are, to encourage, nurture, and challenge them along the path, and occasionally witness amazing results. I have also seen this happen in the rooms of AA, where many unbelieving people enter and, without any proselytizing, end up on their knees in a powerful relationship with the God of grace. So I have come to see the parish church as being a place with wide doors, where we refuse to moralize, threaten, or cajole people into "accepting the Lord Jesus Christ as their Lord and Savior." For me, the line between religious and secular has to be removed to help people name the God who has been engaged with them from the start. This isn't a cookie-cutter approach that cheapens the Christian walk and makes God appear silly. As an Anglican, I believe that God's revelation continues to unfold. Scripture is still being written in our lives today. That's why we can call it the "Living Word of God." The parish's job is to provide space where members can identify and tell their stories of God's activity in their lives. We have done this in my parish for several years, holding story-telling dinners where a person shares his or her autobiography and identifies the places where God has been particularly present. So the Bible continues to be written in my life and in the lives of others. Barbara Crafton says, "If God is as large as we say, there must be many things about God that we don't know yet and can never know, while we live on this earth, since so many things of God are beyond the earthly. If God is free, no place on earth is beyond the divine reach, and we are probably not the gatekeepers of God's activity. Glorying in God's wisdom and humble about our own, we walk forth into the world curious, without assuming ahead of time that we know what we will find."[2] St. Barnabas has become a grace-filled, inviting, open community that rejoices in welcoming individuals of deep faith, agnostics, a few atheists, a few Jews, a Buddhist, a Muslim, and a whole array of others who are growing by grace, not out of fear or law. The depth of faith I find in these parishioners validates our mission and God's immeasurable love as "the hound of heaven." The Church's job is to get out of the way and let God be experienced.

An Interfaith Trip to Israel

One of the great joys of my ministry has been developing a close friendship with the rabbi of a nearby conservative synagogue in Dobbs Ferry, New York. In October 1994 we invited Rabbi Barry Kenter to lead a series called *Getting to Know Our Neighbors: A Look at Our Roots*. The series was a tremendous hit and led to a relationship between our two clergy families as well as our congregations. As our friendship deepened, Barry and I began thinking about our two congregations taking a joint trip to Israel. The Jews and Christians alike had some misgivings. Would the Jews join us in visiting Christian sites? Would the Christians try to convert the Jews? Would we be able to break through our fear and embrace each other in trust and love?

The voyagers on this thirteen-day trip, made up of clergy and their wives and a total combined Jewish-Christian group of twenty-five, had not all known each other prior to this experience. There was the usual polite but distant and cautious posturing of Christians and Jews as each group looked at the other across the divide of our traditions.

We Christians were aware that we embraced both Hebrew scripture and the New Testament but that our Jewish brethren did not share the Gospel with us. For the first three days, the Jews seemed nervous with our worship and with visiting Christian sites. We Christians were amazingly at ease celebrating the Shabbat dinner and liturgy with the Jews. We asked many questions and were genuinely interested in learning about Judaism. They, however, seemed less interested in learning about Christianity. On Ash Wednesday, at a traditional Jordan River baptismal site of Yardenit near the northern shore of the Sea of Galilee, we Christians observed the Ash Wednesday Liturgy and reaffirmed our baptismal vows. Several Jews observed and stayed for the whole liturgy. Finally they began engaging with us. Some made comments such as "Your Ash Wednesday rite is so similar to the one we use at Rosh Hashanah;" "Your baptismal rite feels like a Jewish one," and "I like your approach to doctrine. You, like us, wear it like a loose garment, not like fundamentalists." Then came the most important question, a real zinger. "Are you angry at us Jews for killing Jesus?" Certainly a disturbing accusation, one often leveled against the Jews by Christians, who had at points in their history sought terrible revenge because of this belief. Dialogue had now begun.

Much laughter followed in the days we were together, a mark of the sense of safety and trust that we had achieved. We were now free to let down our hair with each other, play, pray, and be open with one another. We traveled across Israel, from Banias (Caesarea-Philippi) in the Golan Heights in the North to Capernaum to Safed, Megiddo, Nazareth, Jericho, to the Dead Sea and Masada, through the Negev Desert to Eilat in the southern tip, and then north to Tel Aviv as "a new family," learning not to judge or minimize differences. Rather, we learned to understand, respect, and learn from each other. We knew we belonged together as fellow travelers on the earth and were able to share an enormous common pool of tradition. Genuine friendships were established, symbolized by our planting trees in Jerusalem in the Hadassah National Forest.

We Christians were tremendously impressed by the celebration of the Jewish Sabbath, beginning Friday night. Many shops begin closing by Friday noon, and the Sabbath continues until sunset Saturday night. It is a whole mindset that we Christians may have shared a hundred years ago, now all but lost today. *Shabbat* is seen as a time of rest and remembrance of the Jews' dependence on the creator and sustainer of life. It is seen as a family time. Parents bless each child by laying hands on their heads during the *Shabbat* dinner. It is a time to restore balance in life, which the rest of the week makes necessary. Many Jews sacrifice shopping, work, transportation, cooking, washing clothes, working, turning on radio or TV, and using the computer or phone. These are very real and practical reminders of whom we belong to. Many of us felt envious of this high doctrine of the sabbath and certainly were reminded that we Christians need to return to regular Sabbath time and to Scripture, the sourcebook of our faith.

We were also struck by the very clear and constantly reinforced Jewish identity. In their rituals and lifestyles, there are many reminders each day and week of the covenant relationship God has with the Jews, of Jewish suffering in history. and of solidarity with all Jews worldwide.

At the same time, some of us were struck by the catholic (universal) nature of the New Covenant, of Jesus being "a perfect sacrifice for the sins of the whole world." Ours is an inclusive religion. This powerful awareness overcame me as I received Holy Communion at Christ Church near the Jaffa Gate in Jerusalem on our first Sunday. I thought about the ultimate battle between good and evil having been played out just a few yards from where we were sitting. Tears came to my eyes.

Rabbi Kenter spoke to his congregation shortly after our return, saying, "We returned as a community recognizing differences and similarities, recognizing those ties which unite and bind us to one another as creatures of God, mutually respectful of the very theological differences which distinguish each of our faith communities. We returned bonded and inextricably bound the one to the other, connected by a shared love of the land, people and state of Israel, a delight in falafel and shwarma, united by shared belief in the fatherhood of God and the brotherhood of man."

This was a unique pilgrimage, one inspired by God, who is calling us to discover each other and realize that stereotypes and misconceptions may be broken down and that we may clarify our own faith. We all changed by living and traveling together. We have become a bit more honest, open, and appreciative of each other.

Moving Beyond Tolerance

In doing interfaith work, I have come to realize that mere tolerance is not sufficient. It may prevent people from killing each other, but it does not teach us a great deal, and we are not changed if mere toleration is the primary goal. In John 10:16, St. John quotes Jesus as saying, "I have other sheep not of this fold."

Our history as Christians is peppered with acts of intolerance, yet I do believe that Christianity was ever meant to be this way. I want to be very clear: I am a committed Christian and, at the same time, do not believe that my acceptance of people of other faiths without attempting to convert them in any way compromises my Christianity. I believe that God's love revealed in the face and person of Jesus is for the *whole* human family and that all people are made in the image and likeness of God. I claim the power of God's revelation in Jesus, and at the same time, I recognize God's revelation in Judaism and Islam as places where God's truth resides.

Bishop Mark Sisk says, "The difficulty of [interfaith] conversations is that when a person is convinced that they, and they alone, possess the truth, they effectively isolate themselves. This insulating layer of self-certainty cuts them off from real conversation and the potential which it always holds out. However, there is an antidote, a way forward, and that way forward is courage. Any person who truly believes that they have a monopoly on the truth can be challenged to find the courage to share that truth with another, in respectful conversation. In that process of conversation the possibility of mutual engagement is always present. It is that mutual engagement that holds the promise of people meeting as human beings who share in a desire to find the truth that we all seek."[3]

A fascinating article appeared in the *New York Times* on January 12, 2002. It was an interview by writer Gustav Niehbuhr with the president of Union Theological Seminary in New York, the Rev. Dr. Joseph Hough. It was entitled "Acknowledging That God Is Not Limited to Christians." I'm sure that this was shocking to some Christians, but it was validation for what I had come to believe. I called Joe, and we had a wonderful conversation. He calls for the development of a new theology for the way Christians understand other faiths. He is not calling for a melding of all traditions into one, but "for the affirmation of the universal and saving revelation of God that is made concrete in several great religious traditions." As a Christian, he concluded "that the revelation of God's face in Jesus Christ is central and decisive for me." Saying this does not make other religions inferior to Christianity. The Christian enterprise is compelled to bear witness to the truth we have received. Yet sometimes Christian scripture presents problems.

"No One Comes to the Father but by Me"

There is no doubt that one of the greatest stumbling blocks in interfaith dialogue is found in John's Gospel.[4] Immediately after declaring himself to be the way, the truth and the life, Jesus says, "No one comes to the father but by me." This passage has proven a major stumbling block in interfaith dialogue. It certainly, at least on the surface, looks like a lot of people are lost unless they acknowledge the centrality of Jesus. Hell must be full by now! Christians often use this passage as a weapon with which to attack their opponents and knock them out with the threat of hellfire. Many Christians use this passage as a litmus test in interfaith dialogues that are often little more than monologues. Let me hasten to tell you that Jesus wasn't talking about Judaism, Islam (which didn't exist in his day),

Hinduism, or Buddhism. Jesus was speaking only to his own disciples, that tiny band of followers. John is most likely putting words in Jesus' mouth here and making a joyful proclamation to this early religious community that God has revealed himself decisively in the incarnation of Jesus. This claim is announced from the opening lines of John's Gospel in John 1:18—"No one has ever seen God; it is God the only son who is close to the Father's heart, who has made him known." The Christmas story of God's entrance into human flesh in Jesus becomes for the early Christian community the tangible sign of God's love for the world. When Jesus says "no one," he doesn't mean the whole world, merely "none of you" (his disciples). The claim of these early Christians does, in a way, place a distance between them and their Jewish origins. This is a confessional statement of this particular faith community, which has come to believe the truth and the life have been revealed in a unique way. What we as Christians claim in this passage is that Jesus is the fullest revelation of God that we know. The trite proclamation by people of other religions as well as Christians is, "All roads are the same, so go shopping for your brand of religion." I think this is utter nonsense. Bishop Michael Ingham, Anglican Bishop of Vancouver, says, "Openness to a variety of religious practices is dangerous without the security of a grounded religious identity. You need to have a safe home in order to go traveling."[5] We, as Christians, can embrace Jesus as the way, the truth, and the life and as a unique revelation of God for us without telling others that their religion is false. Ours is a way of love and not of arm-twisting. The Christian faith is best shared by attraction rather than promotion.

Interfaith Becomes Personal

Two years after graduating from college and moving back to New York from Boston, our youngest daughter, Amanda, met a Turkish Muslim who was working for his masters degree in art and design at the Pratt Institute in New York City. He moved to London to pursue his PhD, and their relationship became even more serious. They were engaged in 2003; he returned to New York, and they were married at St. Barnabas in 2004. Judy and I liked Dogan very much, but I soon came to realize that there is a quantum leap from doing interfaith work and *being* interfaith. It is ultimately necessary to make the abstract concrete or to bring the intellectual and the emotional together. In the union of Amanda and Dogan, God confirmed for me that the interfaith chapter in my life was more than a passing fancy; it is a true calling. God is very clever and creative!

About a year after Dogan and Amanda were married, the four of us sat in front of a computer and spent two hours speaking with Dogan's parents, his brother and sister-in-law, his sisters, and their husbands and children in their Istanbul home. Even though we had no common language, it was amazing how much we were able to share with each other through humor and facial expression and hand movements. At one point, Dogan's brother, who is a police sergeant in Istanbul, was sitting beside his mother, whose head was covered by a hijab. He said to us, "I can make my mother a Christian in a second." He quickly pulled off her head scarf, and all of us broke into hysterical laughter. The words of the dean of my seminary a few months later resonated in helping me appreciate what had become our international, interfaith family. He had said that "communities are not created by rules, uniformity is the basis of prejudice, not fellowship."[6]

9/11

Irvington sits on the shores of the Hudson River, just twenty miles from midtown Manhattan. September 11th was a crystal-clear day. We had good friends from Australia visiting us. I was in my office next door to the rectory when I received a call from a parishioner in the City, telling me that a plane had hit one of the World Trade Center towers. Soon Emily, our daughter called from Australia, where she was studying pre-med, to tell us that the first tower had just collapsed. We were watching our television just a few miles from the scene, and Emily, around the world, had seen it first; New York was on a two-minute delay. As we talked with Emily, we watched the tower collapse. We switched to Fox Cable News, where our parishioner and youth group leader Jon Scott, the morning anchor, was trying to make sense of what he was witnessing on his monitor. Jon suddenly announced that the second tower had been hit. Then the dreadful truth became apparent—this was a terrorist attack. Judy and I went with Carol and Eric, our Australian friends, to Riverside Park in Irvington, where we could look south down the Hudson River to Manhattan and see the dense smoke billowing from the World Trade Center site. Suddenly, to our horror, we watched the second tower disappear in a cloud of dust. Later in the day, we learned that a parishioner's son-in-law, Ted Hennessy, had been a passenger on American Airlines Flight 11 and that Michael Bane, who had grown up in St. Barnabas, was in the same tower hit by Ted's flight. Although they did not know each other, their lives were joined in one dreadful moment of unspeakable violence. Later, we learned about another Irvington man, Robert Speisman, who died on the plane that hit the Pentagon. For us and for all Americans, our world had suddenly shifted in its orbit.

In the days that followed, a number of disturbing hate crimes were perpetrated against Muslims in the New York area. One such incident happened in a neighboring village when a man screamed insults to a shopkeeper, calling him "one of those goddamn Muslims." The shopkeeper was, in fact, a Sikh. Soon after this incident was reported in our local paper, a young mother and parishioner, Julia dePeyster, deeply disturbed by such stories, searched the yellow pages of the Westchester County Phone directory and located an area mosque. She called to tell them that she was upset by the backlash attacks on Muslims and wanted them to know that she, as a Christian, would stand in solidarity with them and would have her Episcopal church pray for them on Sunday. She then called to tell me what she had done. I remember being astounded that she would take such initiative and reach out in this courageous and kind way. As we talked on the phone, I remember telling her that I knew little of the tenets of Islam. In the days that followed, I called the same mosque that Julia had contacted earlier and asked if they would send a group to meet with us at St. Barnabas and share a bit of their faith with us.

Day of Understanding I

On October 1, 2001 some thirty guests arrived for our 10:00 AM service. There were teenagers and men and women, most of the latter with heads covered, in the group. The congregation was invited to join in a dialogue with these guests in order to understand Islam better and to take a step away from turning hurt into hate in the aftermath of the terrorist attacks. I invited a young Muslim man to intone appropriate verses from the Koran at the beginning, middle, and end of our worship service, and these verses were then translated into English. His opening intonation was from Surah 94: "With every difficulty there is relief." The congregation was in absolute silence. For the first time, Arabic music from another culture was permeating the stone walls of our old church, asking for understanding, respect, and for a place at the table of faith.

Dr. Muhjabeen Hassan is a Pakistani plastic surgeon who had been in the United States for twenty-four year, and some of her patients are my parishioners. In place of my normal sermon, we had a talk from Dr. Hassan. She was clear, direct, humorous, and gracious, explaining the tenets of her faith. She opened with a prayer from the Prophet Moses, asking God to make her speech clear. Muslims, she told us, are monotheists who hold great respect for twenty-six specific great religious figures, including Moses and Jesus, and who also believe in heaven and judgment. Muslims believe that Prophet Mohammed is the final prophet of God. She was clear that Islam leaves no room for such actions as the terrorist attacks on 9/11 and that suicide is totally forbidden. She concluded with a passage from the Koran: "We have formed you into nations and tribes not to convert or kill but to reach out to others with understanding."

After the service, nearly two hundred people moved into the parish hall for a Q & A session and coffee. I have never felt such excitement and electricity in the air before or since; there was a palpable sense of openness, charity, and acceptance. We were eager to come to a fundamental understanding of Islam and to be told that the 9/11 attacks were crimes against humanity and Islam. The Muslims requested that we meet again and include Jews. Dialogue continued for over an hour. Even after officially closing the program, Muslims and parishioners continued to engage in vibrant conversation.

Day of Understanding II

On Sunday, February 10, 2002, we took the next step in sponsoring a Second Day of Understanding, this time including our Jewish brethren. This was a gathering of the three Abrahamic faiths. I shared the experience I had had a few weeks earlier with then-President Khatami of Iran, who spoke to religious leaders at the Cathedral of St. John the Divine at the request of Bishop Mark Sisk, the Episcopal Bishop of New York. Khatami had gone to the United Nations asking for a "dialogue among civilizations," which, he said, was the only hope for our world. Little would we know that his promising reforms would be squashed by reactionary, myopic clerical leaders and that within five years, Iran would face a standoff with the West over nuclear weapons.

The purpose of this second gathering at St. Barnabas was to explore what we had in common as well as our differences and discover a vision for working together. A panel of seven explored the place of Abraham in each of our faiths, placing each religion in historical context. We also looked at how each tradition deals with prejudice, bigotry, and defamation. After an animated and in-depth two hours, I concluded, "I thank you, my Muslim and Jewish brethren, for showing me the other faces of God, the other facets of the Divine. I believe that God sees us all as his beloved children. May this be only the first step of our working together. Peace, shalom, salaam."

The Center for Jewish-Christian-Muslim Understanding

In the two Days of Understanding, the seeds were planted for the creation of a permanent organization that would promote dialogue, understanding, and friendship among the Abrahamic communities. Wright Salisbury was then a parishioner. His son-in-law was killed on Flight 11. Wright spoke to me about continuing the relationship we had started to develop. A small group of us, including Jews, Christians, and Muslims, met informally in the weeks that followed to form the Center for Jewish-Christian-Muslim Understanding (CJCMU). This organization later became more than a program of the Church of St. Barnabas. It has become a tax-free, independent educational corporation.

Prejudice and instances of hostile backlash against Muslims continued. A year after 9/11, three Selden, Long Island, New York teens attacked a Pakistani woman and her fifteen-year-old son when the mother and young man were closing their Tandoori Cottage Restaurant.

"Are you terrorists? Are you connected to Bin Laden?" they asked. They went on: "*You* blew up the World Trade Center Towers!" A larger group in the parking lot egged them on.

The village of Irvington invited me to speak at a memorial service held in its Riverside Park on the first anniversary of 9/11. Franklin Graham and the late Jerry Falwell had each made some shockingly negative comments about Islam being an evil religion. I stood up to an audience of some five hundred people and condemned their comments as a Christian and as president of the Center, receiving a lengthy, standing ovation. The next week a sharp letter of criticism appeared in our local newspaper saying that I had hijacked the event, and who did I think I was to criticize other well-meaning Christians? My comments, however, provoked much discussion and initiated many phone calls and much dialogue. At least people were involved and passionately critical of the obvious ignorant and irresponsible prejudicial comments by two of America's well-known preachers. The effect was heartening and would point the way for the Center's mission to take shape. The board that governs the Center realizes that it won't change the world but is committed to the ripple effect produced by its programs. Each program has the power to affect those who attend, who in turn can have an influence on those in their own individual spheres of influence. We are now, some seven years later, seeing great fruits of our labor in Westchester County.

From the beginning, our goal has been to deal with moderates in each of our religions. We distance ourselves from those, whether Jewish, Christian, or Muslim who are dogmatic and who are not open to learning from the other faiths. I've heard many from each faith make disturbing comments about the others, comments that make dialogue difficult from the start.

"The Jews blew up The World Trade Center."

"It is the Christian's obligation to try to convert Jews and Muslims."

"Muslims are only interested in establishing an Islamic world."

"We were here first, and this is our country."

As a Christian, I do find that in these days of tension, we have a particular role in helping Jews and Muslims sit down at the table and have an honest, respectful dialogue about some very hot issues. This is beginning to happen, and I rejoice. While in Atlanta last year, where I performed a wedding, I was shocked at the reaction of a number of people to our Center for Understanding. "Why would you want to work with Jews and Muslims?" asked a respected member of the community. The idea of interfaith dialogue made a number of people noticeably uncomfortable.

Our board of directors spent the first two years focused on our commonalities as the three faiths of Abraham. There is safety in sticking to the positive, at least until trust is developed and individual intentions are tested. Finally, on a car ride to Drew University to attend a national, interfaith event, four of us from the board began to take a new step in discussing our differences. A Muslim board member began, "I don't understand this Jesus-is-God thing at all." That was a breakthrough for more honest, open discussions of each other's faiths, a dialogue that continues. We have come to a place of honesty, trust, and genuine love for each other, resulting in few inhibitions. Now, we are even able to joke a bit about each other's religions. There are tensions that arise from time to time, but the underlying desire for understanding and mutual mission sustains us through these moments. It may be the issue of appropriately serving Kosher or Halal food at events or about Muslims speaking out against acts of violence by other Muslims or Christians being ignorant of Jewish/Muslim holy days.

Broadening the Circle

In the fall of 2003, with a few dollars in the bank, CJCMU had a dream of bringing together *The God Squad* and a famous Muslim imam. *The God Squad*, in its twentieth year, is comprised of Father Thomas J. Hartman, a Roman Catholic priest, and Rabbi Marc A. Gellman. Father Hartman and Rabbi Gellman are syndicated columnists and New York television personalities who reach over twelve million people in their daily TV show. They are driven by a desire to improve the relationship between Jews and Christians. Their humor and honesty and their affection for each other are winsome and engaging. The Center organized a large event at the Performing Arts Center at the state university at Purchase, New York. We also invited Kuwaiti-born Imam Feisal Abdul Rauf, founder of the American Sufi Muslim Society and co-founder of the Cordoba Initiative, a multi-faith effort to improve the relationship between the Muslim world and the West. This was a new experience for Father Hartman and Rabbi Gellman who had never appeared in such a public forum with a noted Muslim leader. It was also the first county-wide program for the Abrahamic faiths. The program, titled "One Root, Many Branches," was to identify our common origins in Abraham—what brings us together and what separates us. This full-house event opened up doors for the speakers as well as for the participants present. One Muslim woman who came from Valley Forge, Pennsylvania, said, "I'm not always vocal or articulate as I would like to be. This seminar will give me more ammunition to speak my mind." One of the major questions, since 9/11 was a hot topic for the audience, was the issue of why Muslims aren't more vocal in speaking out against acts of extremism, including the terrorist attacks on our country. Imam Rauf was very clear that Muslim leaders have not been given attention in the media and that their comments are severely edited. At the time of the U.S. invasion of Afghanistan, Rauf said that he attempted to persuade a major American newspaper to print a religious edict, signed by dozens of American Muslim leaders, declaring that American Muslims were justified in participating in this war, yet no newspaper would print the release. "I was interviewed by a major national network one month after 9/11," he said, "and I talked about what I did to condemn the attacks. My statement was edited to give the impression that we were not doing anything."

The three religious figures entered into serious dialogue with each other, often with sharp challenges, yet with humor, respect and warmth. Little did we know that *The God Squad* would be so affected by its engagement with Imam Feisal that they would invite him to go on the road with them in a number of other public venues, including CNN. Our seminar, on a shoestring budget, had broadened the circle of conversation and friendship in ways that no one could have predicted.

As time went on, the Center found itself taking to the airwaves on many occasions. We soon had New York television stations asking for interviews as well as receiving coverage in the print media. We went on to produce a series of television programs for local cable stations: "The Faiths of Abraham," "Beyond Tolerance," and "An Island in Time" (Sabbath). We are planning to produce a series of videos that can be used for discussion groups in synagogues, churches, and mosques around the country as well as to establish dialogue groups for ongoing conversation. It is amazing how a simple gesture of reaching out to Muslims, largely out of ignorance, shortly after 9/11, has started many of us on a journey forward that would have seemed like a pipe-dream a few months before.

An Old Model for a New Day

In the Center's board discussions, we kept asking ourselves if there ever had been a model of interfaith cooperation in history that we could hold up for today. One of our Muslim board members, a history buff, suggested that Andalusian Spain provided such an example.

In the Middle Ages Judaism, Christianity and Islam coexisted in the Islamic empire known as al-Andalus, which covered most of the Iberian Peninsula. For the most part, this was an atmosphere of religious tolerance and multiculturalism. It was a period of cross-fertilization and religious freedom that continued for several centuries. Each religion was influenced by the other in terms of theology, music, art, architecture, and even medicine.

Joyce Needleman Stanton, one of our Center board members, speaks eloquently of this period: "Step back in time to a Golden Age, a time when poetry and song flourished ... when intellectual and religious thought found freedom of expression ... step back ten centuries to al-Andalus. There, on the Iberian Peninsula, for a few hundred years, the three peoples of the Book found a way to live together nearly as one. A faint light from this Golden Age still shines down through the years and may serve as a beacon for us today."[7]

The Andalusian model spread its wings and soon took flight, creating great enthusiasm in many patrons of the arts, in religious leaders, in the local Rotary Club, and in several international corporations headquartered in Westchester County. Four months before the November 2005 event, the Center had a bank balance of only $3,000. The program however, would cost $21,000. Another moment of stepping out in faith.

"The Spirit of Andalusia" would include five events and would culminate in a large Music Festival. We began the festival with a program held at the famous Union Church (the Rockefeller Church) with its well-known Chagall windows. The evening was titled "The Power of the Pen." with the guests included Professor Maria Rosa Menocal of Yale, author of *The Ornament of the World* and Professor Ross Brann of Cornell, author of *He Said, She Said: The Andalusi Arabic Love Lyric*. Their presentations were to set the stage for understanding the Andalusian period. The second evening included storytelling and poetry readings by well-known poets and writers, who shared their perspectives on living together in the world. The third event was a lecture, "The Middle East: A Cultural Odyssey," by noted educator Audrey Shabbas, who provided historical background to the festival by focusing on the history and people of the Middle East. Five days later we held a hands-on workshop, "Islamic Art," that walked participants through a maze resembling the streets of Cordoba, where art, geometry, history, and religions converged." The last event before the grand music festival finale was an unusual art exhibit, "Israeli and Palestinian Artists Impressions," which featured artists who rarely meet in real life, displaying their works side by side. This was held at the Rockefeller Preserve, a park and art center on the Rockefeller property, and drew a wide audience.

The culminating event of "The Spirit of Andalusia," and its centerpiece, was held at the Music Hall on the shores of the Hudson River town of Tarrytown, New York, made famous by Washington Irving's stories. Those of us from the Center, who organized this event, knew that we needed at least four hundred people to break even and to pay the musicians. Would it happen? If not, how would we come up with the funds? The preceding events had created a buzz across the county. The Music Festival would include four internationally known groups: the Sharq Arabic Music Ensemble, the Boston Camerata, the flamenco guitarist Jonathan "Juanito" Pascual, and Judith R. Cohen, who is a singer, ethnomusicologist, and specialist in Sephardic music.

The evening arrived. Board members nervously wondered how many would enter the doors. People kept pouring into the Music Hall; many purchased their tickets that evening. The mezzanine and balcony were quickly filled. "God, you are, indeed, gracious!" I whispered. I introduced the Center, and the music began—music from another age and culture wrapped its arms around the audience and formed a community of Jews, Christians, and Muslims, who sat in silence, mesmerized by the stellar performances, applauding each act with passion and appreciation.

The Festival put the Center for Understanding on the map and promised to make the spirit of Andalusia a reality in our day. News began to spread about our work, and soon we began receiving calls from all over the New York metropolitan area from people wanting to be a part of what we were doing. We did not just raise enough money to pay for the whole festival. As with the feeding of the five thousand in Christian scripture, we had several thousand dollars left over. The Center was truly launched and its vision recognized with "The Spirit of Andalusia."

Since the Festival, the Center has held several interfaith youth events, many seminars and discussion groups on a host of topics from "Where Was God in The Tsunami?" to "Freedom of Speech and Minority Rights (The Cartoon Issue)." We also have sponsored a series of visits to houses of worship. For one such series, I took a group of twenty-five to visit the Cathedral of St. John the Divine in New York, where I had been ordained. We were confronted by an exhibit in painting and video from South Africa that had heavy sexual and provocative themes. I was embarrassed, and the Muslims were mortified. Such are the risks! We are establishing a series of dialogue groups in which all the people of Abraham can receive hospitality and dialogue with "the other." These programs are opening unexpected doors of compassion and awareness. The issues that separate us are great, but crossing the thresholds of each other's houses breaks down many stereotypes and begins to dispel fear and anger.

Crossing the Line

In May 2003 I was asked to speak at the funeral of a Jewish woman, Betty, whom I had known for some thirty years. She was a community activist and an expert on Lyme disease in the northeast. Her husband and grown children requested my presence and participation in her funeral. I complied, and as a Christian speaking at the memorial service for a Jewish woman, I was careful to witness to the goodness and love of God without making it faith-specific. A wonderful rabbi conducted the Jewish ritual. The family was very grateful, and I received a number of notes from those who had attended the service, expressing their gratitude for my sensitivity.

Betty's husband Dick, a sometime swimming partner of mine at the local YMCA, developed cancer a few months after his wife's death and died a year later. I received a phone call from his oldest son, saying, "Dad, on his death bed, said that he 'didn't want anyone but Charlie to conduct my funeral.'" The son said, "My siblings and I would like you to do the service in a local Jewish funeral home." I immediately asked which rabbi would take part and was told that "Dad wanted only you."

I must confess that part of me felt that I was doing something unethical and that it would be a breach of interfaith etiquette. After a few hours of struggle, I agreed to officiate. I began the service by saying, "You may wonder how I, a Christian wearing a clerical collar, can officiate at a Jewish funeral. Well, I've asked the same question. All I can tell you is that Dick requested that I do so—and here I am. Jesus was Jewish, and the Jesus Movement in its early days remained within Judaism. Three-quarters of our scripture is Hebrew scripture. So, for Dick, I am here as an Episcopal priest, leaning into my Jewish roots. I hope that you will understand and accept my meager offering this morning."

I read portions of scripture from Isaiah and talked about the Celtic people referring to the space that separates heaven from earth as "thin space," that God holds the living as well as the dead in his love, and that Dick and Betty may well appear in one form or another to his family in the days to come. I said that I believed with every fiber of my being that, in the end, God's love wins out and is victorious over evil and disease and death. I concluded with Job 19:25-27: "I know that my Redeemer liveth and that he shall stand at the latter day upon the earth; and through this body be destroyed, yet shall I see God: whom I shall see for myself and mine eyes shall behold, and not as a stranger."

I was anxious that many Jewish friends attending the service would be angry with me for being a presumptuous intruder. I had the opposite response, thank God! I received many notes from Jews and Christians alike thanking me for the integrity that the service had and for my sensitivity. No, I am not putting out a sign that reads "Interfaith Services Performed." This was an exceptional circumstance.

God's Challenge

I will never forget a photo taken in Indonesia shortly after the devastating tsunami of 2005. It showed a hippopotamus and a tortoise that had adopted each other. They were constant companions 24/7. The moment I saw the picture I realized this was a profound metaphor for humanity. The world is shrinking, and modern communication brings us together as a global community. There are many threats to civilization: nuclear destruction, global climate change, war, poverty, AIDS. It is no longer possible to remain isolated and myopic; we need each other as never before. I believe that God is pointing to the necessity of our interdependence.

In America there are more Muslims now than Episcopalians (5.5 million Muslims and two million Episcopalians). Diana Eck, Harvard professor of Comparative Religion and Director of the Pluralism Project, wrote a seminal book in 2001 that changed my paradigm in interfaith work. The book was *The New Religious America: How a 'Christian Country' Has Become the World's Most Religiously Diverse Nation*.[8] Nowhere else in the world is any other nation dealing with such pluralism and religious diversity. Theodore Roosevelt commented, after seeing Israel Zangwill's 1908 play *The Melting Pot*, that "we Americans are children of the crucible." I believe that the hand of God is in this great American experiment, encouraging us to understand, appreciate, respect, and be open to each other, discovering the face of God. By coming to know and work with our brothers and sisters in other faiths, I come to know my own faith better and discover a facet of God that completes my faith. This is the great challenge before us as Americans. Xenophobia is the enemy of the new community that is forming. This formation is a stretch for all of us, I confess, but there is no other way; the alternative is frightening. If America cannot pull off its great experiment, then the chances for such a thing happening anywhere else in the world are dim. Taking interfaith work seriously is essential because the world is becoming increasingly a small community.

We turn now to a number of other issues that need to be addressed and, in some cases, discarded. What is the essential bottom line of Christianity, and what are some long-held beliefs that we need to shed? How can Christianity relate to our contemporary culture with meaning and passion and stop complaining about the secularization of society? These are crucial issues for the church to address and for us to make clear in our own hearts and minds. Sometimes I feel that the church needs to believe less but to embrace the essentials with more passion.

7

Shifting Sand around the Rock

○ ○

"The wise man built his house on a rock but the ... foolish man built his house upon the sand; and the rain fell, and the floods came and the winds blew ... and it fell."

—*Matthew 7:25-27*

The Rock

When I was growing up on the coast of Maine, my family would often have picnics on Scoodic Point, a rugged peninsula facing the Atlantic Ocean. Scoodic Point is part of Acadia National Park. The beach was strewn with smooth rocks, polished by the tides sweeping the sand repeatedly over them. Even at ten years old, I remember thinking how the rocks remained fixed as the sand washed over and around them.

As a Christian I have come to believe that what God did in Jesus is like the rocks on Scoodic Point. Archbishop Rowan Williams says it well: "Jesus is the face of God turned toward us in history decisively and definitely. The church did not invent the doctrine of the Incarnation: slowly and stumblingly, Christians discovered it."[1] Robert Capon echoes the same theme. He writes, "Jesus is the ultimate sign of what God has always been doing at all times, in all places and for all people"[2] The Incarnation is the centerpiece of the Christian faith, the absolute, essential rock upon which all else is built. The God revealed in the human person of Jesus is a God who is loving and personal; a God who, by coming into human flesh, makes an astounding statement about the goodness of creation and unites the spiritual and material realms as one. We cannot split heaven and earth, secular and religious, because they have been revealed as one unified whole in the person of Jesus Christ, God's unique and ultimate revelation.

The Incarnation becomes the bedrock of the Christian faith. All else must be judged by this centerpiece, including the Church's preoccupation with issues such as correct belief, evangelism, and the ordination of women and gays. All these issues become secondary in importance and often expose Christians as being dogmatic, arrogant, and self-righteous. Just imagine the energy that could be released if we church people would shift our efforts and passion toward truly engaging with the deep hunger in our midst and unveiling the good news of the Christian Gospel. There is a desperate thirst for a God who is personal, involved, and loving. In the church, we often engage in petty arguments instead of with the world itself. Shame on us! More about this in a moment.

On a recent visit to my medical doctor, he began sharing with me his recent near-death experience. On previous occasions he had carefully stayed clear of religious talk, but this time he began to share his view of God with me. It was carefully organized around scientific principles, beginning with the Big Bang theory from which human life accidentally emerged. God, to him, was an abstract principle behind the universe, without personal attributes. I listened, interested in the reason for his unusual openness.

Finally, I said, "Dr. Selby, I agree with you as far as you go, but I'd take it a step further. The Jews discovered that there was only one God and that God was personal. It is in Jesus that Christians came to see even more clearly that God deeply desires to love the world and us into health, and that the God of the Big Bang also knows us by name." I added, "I believe that this truth about God is planted deep in the nature of creation."

He looked out of the window to the Hudson River, sparkling in the bright winter sunlight, and replied, "That would be really good news," and then quickly changed the subject. He had long ago left the church into which he had been born, which was heavy-laden with doctrine to be embraced. Professor Marcus Borg says that "Christianity is a 'way' to be followed more than it is about a set of beliefs to adopt. Practice is more important than "correct" beliefs. Beliefs are not irrelevant; they do matter. But they are not the object of faith. God is the 'object' of commitment—and for Christians, God is known in Jesus."[3]

Living versus Believing

King Solomon said: "Behold, heaven cannot contain thee; how much less this house which I have built."

—I Kings 8:22-30

There are signs of extremism throughout our society. Christian fundamentalists speak authoritatively on behalf of God, with little humility. There is tremendous growth in fundamentalist churches—growth which, I believe, should not seduce us into adopting their values. The fundamentalist movement is fanning flames of rigidity, and in some cases, of hatred around the world. What do these groups have in common?

Many fundamentalists view life and moral decisions in black and white terms; they acknowledge no gray, no ambiguity. Every moral and societal question is given a clear and decisive answer; a declaration of sin is eagerly and forcefully pronounced. I don't know about you, but these people live in a world I find hard to identify with. For me, most moral and ethical decisions are not all that clear and simple. They are often gray in color. My problem with those in both camps of the abortion argument is that they are oversimplifying the issues. In most of the instances known to me when a woman was faced with this decision, the matter was complex and surrounded by extenuating circumstances. We do not have the luxury of seeing these decisions as being purely good or purely evil. In my view, as well as in that of Anglican moral theology, we must often choose between the least of two evils. That's not the easy way, and it's not tidy and clean, but it is reality.

We find it difficult to live with shadow when certainty is offered to us on a silver platter. Watch out, however, for this kind of comfort; it is cheap grace, and it is idolatrous. Don't settle for any answer that is too simplistic, and don't confuse it with truth. God is in charge, and all will be well. Depend on God's grace, and not on an oversimplified, dogmatic, and often unloving position. Pope Benedict XVI, for the second time in three years, has made it clear that the Roman Catholic Church is the true church and that the rest of us are broken, schismatic religious organizations. Why is it necessary for him to continue this theme? The idea that one branch of the church has preserved itself as pure without brokenness is certainly questionable!

The poet Coleridge spoke about Christianity being a way of life rather than a doctrine. In my forty-five years as a priest, I have reconstructed my understanding of the Christian faith several times. In recent years I have come to understand faith as more of a way of living than assent to a set of beliefs. I have come to agree with what St. Augustine said: "Christ is the Journey as well as the Journey's end." John Robinson, the English cleric, used to tell his followers to wear theology like a loose garment, separating essentials from nonessentials.

I want to extol the virtues of ambiguity as a useful tool in pursuing a Christian life. According to Webster's Dictionary, one of the meanings of *ambiguity* is to understand something in two or more senses. We need to learn to live with ambiguity. It eventually makes us wise and reveals the truth to us. Far too often religion promotes itself and its ideas as changeless and fixed. This may provide a sense of security, but the great truths about God are too large to be neatly boxed and wrapped. We hate ambiguity, openness, and things left unresolved, yet ambiguity grants us freedom to discover new shades of truth and added dimensions of the mystery we call God. What we need is grace to live with ambiguity and understand it as valuable. God will not be domesticated or tamed by us. God's truth will eventually reveal itself to the Church, whether the Church is ready to accept it or not. God often nudges us to see the larger picture, and we Christians don't much like that approach.

I believe that a parish church is meant to be a safe place where people can bring their questions and doubts and explore the great mysteries that the Church and life set before them. I have been encouraged in my interfaith work with Jews and Muslims. Neither faith is wedded to "right belief," but rather to "right practice." This is the reason that in both faiths, a whole range of positions can be found on a variety of issues. Observant Jews and Muslims practice their faith by observing the Sabbath and saying their prayers several times a day. This can be called *orthopraxy* or right practice. The Christian mistake, which the church slips into, is called *orthodoxy* or right belief. The Church is often obsessed by protecting what it considers orthodox theology, forgetting that the creeds and doctrines emerged over several decades in the early church and only after battles and divisions.

Karen Armstrong, the English writer on the origins of the Abrahamic faiths, had a Jewish friend who said to her, "You Christians make such a fuss about theology, but it's not important in the way you think. It's poetry, really, ways of talking about the inexpressible. We Jews don't bother much about what we believe. We just do it instead."[4] Although beliefs are important, we must be reminded that they are not the object of faith. We Christians need to learn to hold the creeds in one hand while approaching God with the other, never telling God what the limits of truth are to be. This approach to faith is not fuzzy-minded or wishy-washy but an honest, humble, and exciting avenue to God and truth. The parish where I have served as rector for thirty-six years is a dynamic community of faith where no questions or doubts are off limits. The freedom to ask questions and challenge tenets of faith has not led to a bland, faceless, all-things-to-all-people milieu. Rather, this freedom has led people into a deeper and more passionate relationship with God and each other and a serious engagement with the needs of the broader community. I believe that we can be deeply faithful without being pious or rigid, which leads to an honesty that is attractive and nurturing.

Interpretation of Scripture

"You have your heads in your Bibles constantly because you think you'll find eternal life there. But you miss the forest for the trees. These Scriptures are all about me! And here I am, standing right before you, and you aren't willing to receive from me the life you say you want." John 5:39-70 in Eugene Peterson's contemporary Scripture translation, *The Message*, is a paraphrase of Jesus' words and accents their pointedness.

Fundamentalism and biblical literalism emerged in the twentieth century and now pit Christians against each other. The approach to interpretation of Scripture is at the core of so many battles within the church today. One belief is that Scripture, which for Christians is composed of Hebrew Scripture and the New Testament, is a closed revelation. This concept suggests that God is no longer revealing himself to us. This represents a static view of God and of Scripture itself. I believe that God enters into a partnership with us in revelation. Therefore, scripture is not unchanging but dynamic, alive and expansive for each new generation. Brother Tobias Haller says, "It is clear that the plain text of Scripture alone, without the interpretation and authority of the Church in response to the needs of the world, does not serve well as a simple rule-book for right and wrong, and, more importantly, has only rarely been employed in this way. Moreover, upon many occasions in which Bible texts have been employed to 'settle the matter' the decisions reached are judged in subsequent generations to have been erroneous or worse."[5]

We are not meant to *believe in* scripture, but rather to *give our hearts to it*, which is the meaning of the Latin word for *credo*.

The Gay Issue

The consecration of the first openly gay person, Gene Robinson, as Bishop of New Hampshire in 2003, set off a firestorm within the Anglican world. The Episcopal Church in the USA is a part of this Anglican world. A few dozen parishes and a couple of dioceses have withdrawn from the Episcopal Church and become part of an alternative network.

The use of scripture as proof texts in dealing with issues such as slavery, the place of women, polygamy, divorce, stem cell research, atomic weaponry, and the gay issue is a misuse of scripture to serve our own ends. Scripture had no understanding, for example, of sexual orientation and genetics as we do today.

The Hebrew scriptures often address the pagan practice of worshipping and deifying sex in order to pacify the fertility gods who provided the fruits of the earth. The issue was clearly idolatry. There were female and male prostitutes who were instruments in pagan temple worship.

In I Corinthians 6:9-10, St. Paul is quite clear: "Make no mistake, no fornicator or idolater, none who are guilty either of adultery or of homosexual perversion ... will possess the kingdom of God." What this translation calls "homosexual perversion" is an aggregation of two words in the original Greek, described in the King James Version as "effeminate" and "abusers of themselves with mankind." Nearly all contemporary translations combine these into one word. Paul, in Romans 1:26-27, refers to shameful passions. "Their women have exchanged natural intercourse for unnatural and their men in turn, giving up natural relations with women, burn with lust for one another; males behave indecently with males ..." (New English Bible). The problem is again idolatry in Rome which was the setting for this letter.

I have visited Corinth twice. The tour guide always points out the hill overlooking the Christian ruins. It was there that a large pagan temple existed in Paul's day. Preaching to Christians at the bottom of the hill, he would point upward and condemn both female and male prostitution and point to the one and only God who did not sanction such idolatry.

There is no reference in Paul to homosexual orientation; certainly there is no knowledge of the emerging genetic theory we understand. Homosexuality is not mentioned in the Ten Commandments or by Jesus. It is striking that homosexuality should receive no explicit mention if it really is serious enough to keep one from enjoying the full benefits of God's love. So, we have to be careful not to misuse passages as proof texts, which is often done; the evidence will not support this approach.

Recently I visited a woman in the hospital who was from a medical family. She was extremely distressed by the Episcopal Church's action and strongly held that homosexuality was a chosen lifestyle that was sinful. I thought for a moment and asked her, "If science proves tomorrow that people are born gay, that it is genetic, how would you feel?"

She paused a moment and said, "Then I would have to change the way I see things."

There is an increasing amount of evidence that, in fact, many people are born homosexual and have nothing to say about it, as is evidenced by a new study involving twins. If medical science proves that our sexuality is a given, at least in most cases, which I believe it is doing, then how does that affect our theology? I believe that wherever truth is, there is God. In John 14:6, Jesus said, "I am the way, the truth and the life." In John 18:38, he says, "I have come into the world to be a witness to the truth."

If someone is born gay or somewhere along the line comes to the realization that he or she is gay, then we need to make room for full acceptance in our theology and in our church life. The repeated idea that homosexuality is a choice is difficult to justify in our day.

The Church is obligated to accept gay people as full members, just as heterosexuals are accepted, and this is the official position of the Episcopal Church. We must hasten to add, however, that both groups must be held to the same moral standard. No one gets off the hook for immoral behavior as Christians. We must scorn the outrageous, acting-out sexual behavior by Madonna, Britney Spears, Paris Hilton, and others as well as that sometimes seen in Gay Pride parades. We must condemn the misuse of sex and relationships in our society for both heterosexuals as well as gay people. We are called to have respect for human beings and not to use them as objects. Sex must be disciplined by love and respect. It is meant to be sacramental, "an outward and visible sign of an inward and spiritual grace." All Christians are called to love and commitment, fidelity and faithfulness in relationships. The Church condemns promiscuity, whether by heterosexuals or homosexuals. We must speak up against licentiousness in heterosexual and homosexual populations and not worry about being politically correct. Because sexuality is such a sensitive area of human life, it has the potential to encourage self-centeredness, self-gratification, and self-deception.

Recently there was a proposal before the General Convention of the Episcopal Church, the official governing body that meets every three years, to write liturgies for the blessing of homosexual/lesbian committed relationships. There was a recognition that such services do exist in a variety of dioceses without any official approval. The Church blesses a variety of things: fleets of ships, houses, animals, and institutions. Therefore, why not invoke God's blessing upon a permanent, committed, faithful gay relationship that will bring stability to society? I took part in such a ceremony a number of years ago. It wasn't understood as marriage, but the Church's blessing of a committed relationship. A Lutheran minister did the blessing, and I offered a prayer.

Barbara Crafton leaves the doors open for a variety of positions in light of the raging controversy in the Episcopal Church. "Consensus never emerges from church councils. It grows afterwards. We have always lived without consensus. Unity has not meant uniformity of opinion among us since there has been a Church of England. It was Queen Elizabeth I who said, 'I have no wish to open windows into men's souls," erecting a standard of freedom of conscience that has endured among us.' There are Anglicans who are more Protestant in their religious orientation; others are more Catholic. Some are conservative and defend their position in Scripture. Others point with equal certainty to the burden of argument within Scripture and its study, within which they find support for a liberal position. Our church knows that everyone has a lens—you cannot see without one, and every lens is different. We don't all see the same thing, and we don't see things in the same way. That's OK. Now we live in what we have done and walk a while to see how it fits. Now hearts and minds follow where law has led—or find that they cannot. The story continues, either way."[6]

It is absurd to think that the Church hasn't had gay clergy, probably from the beginning. This is not a new phenomenon; we are only now becoming honest about it and mindful of it. Providing equal rights to gay people is very important, as is providing full membership in the ordained life of the church. One's character is always an important criterion for selection. I'm certainly not saying that homosexuality is an insignificant issue to wrestle with, but it is to our shame that this issue is tearing Anglicanism apart. For heaven's sake, there are also other crucial issues facing the church. We are spending an inordinate amount of energy and focus on this single issue while millions of our people are spiritually starving. Let each camp allow the other to live with its position, trusting that over time God will make the issue clear. The early Church allowed such differences of belief without crucifying those who didn't agree with it.

To Hell with Hell

It was the fall of 1987, and the well-known English evangelist Canon Bryan Green came to lead a mission (a Christian teaching series) at a nearby church. I had heard that he was dynamic, a straight shooter, and contemporary. I had struggled for years with the concept of eternal hell and had long questioned its reality in light of the love of God, which, I believed, could not be resisted in the end. Bryan was a vital man with bushy, white eyebrows and a naughtiness that I found attractive.

About thirty minutes into his address, he removed his glasses, leaned forward on the lectern, and said, "Now I want to talk with you about this hell rubbish." He went on to quote Christian scripture as well as early church fathers such as Origin, St. Jerome, and St. Gregory of Nyssa, who all affirmed God's ultimate victory over evil and the restoration of all things. He continued to point to contemporary Christians who held the same position: William Temple, Robert Runcie, and Hans Kung. He said, "In the end, I hope that God will save the worst of us, and that hell will be empty; otherwise, what a terrible defeat for God's love." He continued, saying, "I have come to understand a need for 'purgatory.' When I face God in his love everything will be known about me. Purgatory is the experience after death of the love of God face to face, where we will be judged by God's love and welcomed in. Dear friends, no one goes on God's garbage heap!"[7] Bryan visited St. Barnabas three times in the following years and always brought clarity, simplicity, and inclusiveness to the Gospel of love. I spent an afternoon with him in Oxford a couple of years after his first visit to Irvington. He made the power of God's love in Christ's life, death and resurrection palpable and ever so attractive. When I left Oxford, boarding a train back to London that day, I was exhilarated and euphoric. I pondered the core message of the Bible as being Love and realized that it must take precedence over individual passages. This was a moment of clarity that I had sought for many years.

On the Sunday after Saddam Hussein was executed, we prayed for him at St. Barnabas during our Sunday Eucharist, which raised many eyebrows. A few had the courage to ask why. My answer was that no one is ever completely out of the reach of God's saving love. I said to one person, who was most disturbed by our prayer for Hussein, that if the devil himself appeared at our altar rail, I would give him Holy Communion; the call to withhold God's embrace and grace was not mine to make. Yes, I believe that Hitler, Stalin, and Saddam are in heaven. If this offends your sense of justice, I would remind you that God's justice and love are different sides of the same coin.

I recently read the amazing story of Bishop Carlton Pearson, who grew up in a ghetto near San Diego, in a strict Pentecostal home. He comes from a long line of ministers. He became an important part of the Oral Roberts ministry and later built a mega church, Higher Dimensions, that drew as many as five thousand people every Sunday. In 1996 Pearson had a revelation while in prayer that turned his life and ministry upside down. He gave up a belief in eternal hell and started preaching the all-embracing love of God. This meant a new view of scripture and an inclusive Gospel that welcomed gays, atheists, Jews, and Muslims as already saved. The result was that his congregation turned against him, and the Pentecostal community made him an outcast. He lost his reputation, his church, and his livelihood. His story is telling in that it highlights religion's desperate need to preserve the doctrine of hell as a tool for control.[8]

Yes, I believe that everyone goes to heaven. Hell as estrangement from God, from self and others, is real but is restricted to this earthly realm. I also believe that society experiences judgment in this life but, in the end, will be restored to wholeness, which is the meaning of the word salvation. Hell has generally been treated as a Christian doctrine, yet I see it as shifting sand and not of the essence. A new interpretation, or rather a corrective one, is long overdue!

No hymn of Christiandom says it better than the one written by Frederick William Farber in 1862.

> "There's a wideness in God's mercy
> Like the wideness of the sea;
> There's a kindness in his justice,
> Which is more than liberty.
>
> For the love of God is broader
> Than the measure of man's mind;
> And the heart of the Eternal
> Is most wonderfully kind."

So, I'll see you in heaven, compliments of God's grace!

Ghosts and the Communion of Saints

I believe that there is one unified reality and that heaven and earth are not separable. Heaven intersects this earthly realm constantly. This is the reason we need to clean up our language in the use of such phrases as *physical versus spiritual* or *secular versus religious*. There is only one reality that surrounds us, supported by our belief in God's entrance into human flesh in Jesus.

St. Barnabas Church is in the midst of Washington Irving country. In fact, Irving was a close literary friend of William McVickar, the founder and first rector of the parish from 1852-1867. They often sat before the rectory den fireplace for hot toddies on Sunday afternoons. Prior to going to St. Barnabas in 1972, I thought of ghosts as belonging to the English and associated with Halloween.

Some five years after moving into the rectory, our two-year-old daughter Amanda began waking up from her naps and asking, "Mommy, why doesn't that woman ever speak to me?" Amanda described an elderly woman with her grey hair in a bun, sitting in a rocking chair and knitting. She would simply look at Amanda and stare. This happened repeatedly. Believing this to be a sweet imaginary friend, we said, "Try to go back to sleep." In 1983, when Amanda was eight, I brought home a book on the history of the rectory to show Judy. It was written by Isabel K. Benjamin, the daughter of the Rev. William H. Benjamin. Benjamin had been the second rector of St. Barnabas, who served for forty years and lived in the rectory until he died in 1907. Amanda saw the book opened to a picture of Mrs. Isabel Rodgers Benjamin, William's wife. Amanda became very excited and screamed, "That's the woman I was telling you about, the woman who used to rock and knit in my room." The text accompanying the photo read, "Often on winter evenings my father and I played checkers or backgammon while my mother knitted or worked on tapestry or made my dresses."

Several years later Judy was sitting in the rectory kitchen late one night while watching television and sorting through papers. Suddenly the head of an elderly woman with her hair in a bun appeared next to the television set and stared at her for several seconds before disappearing.

On another occasion we were in the dining room of the rectory near the downstairs bathroom when, suddenly, the hot water faucet turned on full force. This happened two additional times in the next several months, always when we were at home. After the second incident, I addressed the ghost and said, "Listen, this is too creepy, and I don't like this. Please stop it. This is our home, and we can't live this way. I hope that you'll understand. Thank you very much. Good night." There was one more incident, a few weeks later. I repeated my request, only a bit more forcefully this time, and it has never happened again.

The Church has had its share of ghostly appearances also. When I came to St. Barnabas, Ethel Cook was our oldest member of the parish, born in 1894. She was only thirteen years old when Dr. Benjamin died. Before Ethel died in 1981 at aged eighty-seven she told me a story of being in the church on altar guild duty one morning when she saw Dr. Benjamin appear in his Sunday vestments near the high altar. He stopped, turned toward her, and then walked through the wall into the sacristy where vestments and chalices are kept. Ethel was a very rational, scientific woman, not prone to visions, which made her testimony all the more believable.

In 1990 the church finally installed a sound system with a control cabinet in the back. The system was given in memory of Daniel Rutledge, long-time parishioner, who had served many years at the United Nations. The control cabinet had multiple knobs, switches, and dials, which were always set for the next service before being locked and alarmed. Only one woman, Anne Roberts, who had helped design the system, knew the intricacies of the controls. Several months after the system was installed, we became aware that every time the cabinet was opened all the dials and switches had been changed. About the same time, three seven-day computerized thermostats in the Church were changed to random time settings. We decided that a ghost must be tinkering with those modern electronics. One morning when no one was around, I went into the back of the church, stood by the sound cabinet, and addressed the ghosts.

"Listen, I'm sure that you have been here in the past and that you love this place as much as I do. I have to tell you, however, that these incidents are a real problem for us. Please stop messing with the sound system and the thermostats. Thank you very much. God bless you." That was the last such tinkering to occur. I am grateful to have ghosts with whom we can reason. Soon after this incident, Anne, our sound person, saw a ghost open and walk through the door into the sacristy. The "company of heaven" is, indeed, a reality at St. Barnabas.

Late in 1997, Barbara Wright, a faithful and hard worker in the parish, was climbing stairs in the parish hall. They led to a set of offices and storage areas above. As she neared the top, she sensed a strong presence walking down the stairs past her. She described the feeling as "strange yet normal, even though I couldn't see the person."

In 1999 a new organ was being installed in the church, the gift of Bard and Mary Louise Bunaes. Our brilliant organist-choirmaster, Donald Butt, who has been at St. Barnabas for forty years, helped design the fantastic new instrument. The installation took several weeks as cables, cabinetry, and hundreds of pipes, including state trumpets in the back of the church, were assembled. One warm summer afternoon, Dick Taylor, one of the owners of American Classic Organ Company, was working alone in the church when a thunderstorm moved across the Hudson River toward the church. As darkness fell suddenly upon the church, a strong lightning bolt illuminated the building. Suddenly Dick saw a man in old-fashioned garb standing near him. He ran to the back of the church and turned on all the lights, but found no one there. After that incident he always arrived with his business partner, Mike, by his side.

How do I explain these apparitions? I am happy to say, in our case, all the ghosts are benign and responsive. I do know that at times in my own life, I have felt the clear presence of one of my grandmothers, of my parents, and of my mother-in-law. As a Christian, I am not surprised by these visits. We profess in the Nicene Creed a belief in "the Communion of Saints"—that there is a fine line between heaven and earth. Physicists are beginning to address such mysteries as time and eternity. I find that such a view enriches and expands my rather myopic world view. Why should we think it so strange? Jesus told us about this two thousand years ago in John 14:2: "In my father's house there are many rooms." And in Luke 17:21: "The kingdom of God is in the midst of you." In each Eucharistic celebration, we affirm this in the preface before the Sanctus: "With angels and archangels and with all the company of heaven, who forever sing this hymn to proclaim the glory of your name ..."⁹ To be surrounded by those who have gone before us is to make our existence an experience of community. We are, in fact, part of a large family. The Church gets very nervous about ghosts or those who communicate with the departed. I must admit that there are many who exploit this field, yet there are also many who are tuned in to what many faithful Christians of a previous era used to take for granted. Are we dealing with sand or rock here? I believe we are on solid stone. If the eternal and the earthly are forever bound together in the Incarnation, then our belief in the Communion of Saints is at the heart of what we believe. The concept is exciting and expands our narrow view of what we call reality.

Marketing Christianity

I was ordained a priest in 1963. Until the mid-80s, most new people who entered our church doors had a basic understanding of the Christian story line. They knew about the birth, ministry, passion, death, and resurrection of Jesus. They had heard of the trinity and the sacraments and knew something about prayer. Now, some twenty-five years later, the picture has changed dramatically. Beginning in the 1960s, church going began to become unpopular as most institutions became suspect. The current newcomers grew up in this environment but want their children to have something spiritual. The majority who now venture into our parishes know few rudiments of Christianity; they aren't hostile, just uninformed. To some extent, this is an advantage because we don't have to help people unlearn some misconceptions of the faith they learned as children. Katherine Jefferts Schori, the Presiding Bishop of the Episcopal Church, has it right when she challenges us, "How would you tell the great truths of our faith without using overtly theological language? How would you tell a new neighbor that God loves him or her without measure, and invite him or her to learn more? If we are going to hear that person's story with grace, we have to leave the door open for a while." 10

This is a great challenge for church leaders who have long settled into their explanations of the faith in theological and biblical language. This is a new moment of challenge for clergy, who now must find "secular" images and nonreligious language to convey the great truths about the transforming love of God that the Church holds as central. It is a challenge for us to begin engaging with people in the public square. Kierkegaard told the story of a wasp that landed on his dinner plate one day. He took his knife and cut the wasp in half. To his amazement the wasp kept on eating as if nothing had changed. The church is a bit like this. Even though it is, in many cases being ignored, it keeps right on doing things in the same old way. We need to help the church face the world and not itself. Recently, I led a rather unconventional twelve-week course called "Living the Questions." This approach to the faith was a bit edgy and daring, treating people's questions with great respect. The course encouraged us to look at issues of who Jesus was, the miracle stories, and his death and resurrection through a new pair of glasses. It opened up old doctrines, including the one about understanding scripture to be the inerrant and literal word of God. To some, this was unnerving, but to most it proved to be a refreshing and honest approach. As one of the participants commented, "I feel so relieved to realize that there are a number of ways to understand various elements of Christianity." As a result of this course, many participants became more tuned in to the words of our Sunday liturgy, asking questions and seeking a new framework for understanding the Christian story.

The church can be blind to its own idolatry. Often we confuse the symbols of our liturgy with what they are meant to point to. Liturgy is a vehicle and not an end in itself. The church needs to learn how to open up the great truths without being rigid and pious. Thomas Merton, the great spiritual giant of the twentieth century, knew this well: "A saint is capable of talking about the world without any explicit reference to God, in such a way that his statement gives greater glory to God and arouses a greater love of God than the observations of someone less holy, who has to strain himself to make an arbitrary connection between creatures and God through the medium of hackneyed analogies and metaphors that are so stupid they make you think there is something the matter with religion."[11]

It is important for our churches to embrace and welcome all people: unbelievers, serious questioners, those who are hungry for truth and God, gay people, alcoholics, addicts and those who come out of a vague desire to find meaning. When our doors are wide enough, many enter for a myriad of reasons, yet they find themselves taking the next step once they locate a place in the community of faith. They catch a glimpse of the reality and attractiveness of God and go on to the next step. We, who are in leadership must leave the door wide open but also provide real and honest sustenance once newcomers are settled into the parish. This combination is a sure winner. It takes the world seriously and makes the church relevant to everyday life. When the default mode of a parish church is survival, it is sure death for the church and a depressing advertisement for those who look at us from the outside. We spend far too much energy on who should be admitted to the sacrament of Holy Communion; we politicize the pulpit, essentially disenfranchising those who don't agree with us; we often talk as if the Church and God are synonymous; and we spend our last breath fighting over the issue of homosexuality. We need to clean up our act, put first things first, and return to the God-business which is our calling.

The word for *crisis* in Chinese is made up of two characters: one for *danger* and the other for *opportunity*. This is where the church finds itself in our day. It clearly is in crisis, and this is a dangerous place and moment when its very survival as we have known it is at stake, yet this crisis brings with it a golden opportunity to market the faith in new wrappings. We must make no mistake about it: the Church is in the marketing business, and we must do that business well because we have the greatest product the world has ever known.

God grant us the vision to engage with the world that surrounds us. We walk and live our lives amidst an abundance of sand that shifts under our feet, yet the Rock at the center is the God who loves the secular enough to embrace it in Jesus and to reveal his love for us and for the world in which we live.

Afterword

> *"Religion declined not because it was refuted, but because it became irrelevant, dull, oppressive, insipid. When faith is completely replaced by creed, worship by discipline, love by habit; when the crisis of today is ignored because of the splendor of the past; when faith becomes an heirloom rather than a living fountain; when religion speaks only in the name of authority rather than with the voice of compassion, its message becomes meaningless."*
>
> —*Abraham Joshua Heschel*

How wise Heschel was! The Church has been given the responsibility of safeguarding the Good News of the Gospel, yet it is always in danger of becoming the focus rather than pointing to the incredible truth of what God has done for us in Jesus.

Our life as Christians must remain open, fluid, contemporary, responsive and compassionate while holding up the love that God is. We need to resist being rigid, dogmatic, and overly pious. Our life together should leave ample room for different styles, personalities, and theological positions while safeguarding the truth about the one who is at the center of our life, who makes us a community and holds us together. The church at its best stands for unity in diversity.

Jesus majored in the secular and attacked the split between secular and religious because he understood God as involved in all of life. As Christians we must affirm the profound link between the street and the church, and between earth and heaven. The Church is not a place to hide from the world, but a place where we gather to celebrate God in the world. God doesn't intend for our worlds to collide, but has shown us the solution for bringing them together. This is the greatest gift we have to share with others. I have an astute friend, Barry Seaman, retired writer and editor for *Time*, who says that "Life in the church and in the world bleed all over each other and thus have to be dealt with together."

It is essential for us as Christians to become aware of our own inner splits: between spirit and flesh, religious and secular, and between heaven and earth. Clergy also need to recognize the danger of "two-class thinking," the split between the ordained and the laity. The two orders have their own functions within the Church but they are both players on the same ball team and one is not more important than the other.

The Christian walk can be a bumpy trail, yet the bumps become places of great blessing. Doubt becomes merely another facet of faith, not its opposite, and is to be honored and respected. As with doubt, we meet other dragons on the Christian journey. In God's world, everything becomes grist for the mill, even our desperate moments which have a way of readying us for a discovery of God's power in our weakness. This gift of God's radical grace transforms us from broken people into empowered pilgrims on the road. Our faith begins to take shape as a way of life and not a package of beliefs, a relationship with the living God instead of being mired in rules and empty words. Scripture can come to life and become the living, breathing story of God's presence among us. Along this road we begin to gaze on the love of God and not on the threat of hell. Later we become keenly aware that the whole human family is linked together as God's family, and we are able to expand our views to include "the other," those different from ourselves who may be Jewish, Muslim, Buddhist, or Hindu, and to believe that God has given each of us gifts that the other needs. And finally on our journey we begin to delineate between what is essential Rock and what is shifting sand. This realization is crucial for our survival as well as that of the Church.

The great psychologist Carl Jung said, "Bidden or not bidden, God is present." These words were carved over Jung's front door and also on his tombstone. God doesn't need to be invoked to be present; we only need to make connections, like a child connecting the dots to allow the picture to take shape on the pages of our lives. All of us are given the opportunity, like Mary, to say "Yes" and give our consent to God becoming incarnate in our lives. The Christian journey is about endings and beginnings. The English poet T. S. Eliot captures these transitions.

> "We shall not cease from exploration
> And the end of all our exploring
> Will be to arrive where we started
> And know the place for the first time.
> Through the unknown, remembered gate

When the last of earth left to discover
Is that which was the beginning ..."[1]

There has been a central theme in my life: tearing down the wall that separates life into compartments of religious and secular, spirit and flesh. Coming to this realization changes everything and has given me a new paradigm for living, which I believe *is* the Christian Gospel. I have fought many battles, and I have experienced a collision of worlds throughout my life, but the freeing revelation for me is the knowledge that our worlds do not have to collide. Indeed, salvation is discovered when we bring them together. I have returned to the place where I began my journey, but I see everything with new eyes. Praise God!

Notes

Preface

1. John A. T. Robinson, *Honest to God*, (Louisville, Westminster John Knox Press, 2006).

Chapter One—No Balm in Gilead: Doubt

1. Jon Gorsuch, *An Invitation to The Spiritual Journey*, (Mahwah, NJ: Paulist Press, 1990), 30.
2. American Public Media: *Speaking of Faith*, September 28, 2006.
3. Rowan Williams, *A Ray of Darkness*, (Cambridge, MA: Cowley, 1995), 82.
4. Ibid., 104.
5. Philip Yancey, *Reaching For The Invisible God*, (San Francisco: Harper Collins, 2000), 39.

Chapter Two—Encountering Dragons

1. Sermon preached at The Church of St. Barnabas, Irvington, NY, November 27, 2005.
2. Rowan Williams, *A Ray of Darkness*, (Cambridge, MA: Cowley, 1995), 84.
3. Anne Lamott, *Blue Shoe*, (New York: Riverhead Books, 2002).
4. Desmond Tutu, *God Has A Dream*, (New York: Doubleday, 2004), 17.

Chapter Three—Demythologizing the Priesthood

1. Rowan Williams, *A Ray of Darkness*, (Cambridge, MA: Cowley, 1995), 152.
2. John Sanford, *Ministry Burnout*, (New York: Paulist Press, 1982), 72.
3. Alan Jones, *Sacrifice and Delight*, (San Francisco: Harper, 1992), 55.

4. George Bernanos, *Diary of a Country Priest*, (New York: Carroll and Graff, 1983), 140.

5. Robert K. Massie, Jr., *An Epistle to My Friends and Family*, (Spring, 1981).

6. Karen Armstrong, *The Spiritual Staircase*, (New York, Alfred A. Knopf, 2004), 300.

Chapter Four—Embracing the Secular

1. Alan Jones, *Sacrifice and Delight*, (San Francisco: Harper, 1992).

2. William F. Bellais, *Work and Human Dignity,"* (*The Living Church*, June 20, 2004).

3. Karl Rahner, *Spirit in the World*, (New York: Continuum, 1993), 17.

Chapter Five—Radical Grace

1. Peter Gomes, *The Good Life*, (San Francisco: Harper, 2002), 256.

2. Robert Capon, *The Romance of the Word*, (Grand Rapids: Eerdmans, 1995), 337.

3. Sermon preached at the Church of St. Barnabas, September 16, 2007, by the Rev. Joel C. Daniels.

4. David Steindl-Rast, *Gratefulness, The Heart of Prayer*, (New York: Paulist Press, 1984), 9.

5. Paul F. M. Zahl, *Grace in Practice*, (Grand Rapids, William B. Eerdmans, 2007), 253.

Chapter Six—Neither Jew Nor Greek: Interfaith Dialogue.

1. Alan Jones, *Re-imaging Christianity*, (New York: Wiley, 2005), 24.

2. Barbara C. Crafton, *Let Us Bless the Lord*, (Year One), (Harrisburg: Morehouse Publishing, 2005), 222-3.

3. Mark Sisk, *Can There Be Common Ground?* ("*On Faith*," *Newsweek/Washington Post* Blog, November 15, 2006.)

4. Charles Colwell, "*Is Ours the True Religion?*" *Personal Journey* Magazine. (Primedia, Inc. Fall 2005.)

5. Michael Ingham, *Mansions of the Spirit*, (Toronto: Anglican Book Center, 1997), 62.

6. Ward B. Ewing, *G. T. S. News*, Spring 2006, 6.

7. Joyce Needleman Stanton, board member of the Center for Jewish-Christian-Muslim Understanding, "*Waiting on the Spirit of Andalusia*" Program, November 13, 2005.

8. Diana L. Eck, *New Religious America*, (San Francisco, Harper, 2001).

Chapter Seven—Shifting Sand around the Rock

1. Rowan Williams, *A Ray of Darkness*, (Cambridge, MA: Cowley, 1995), 60.

2. Robert Capon, *The Romance of the Word*, (Grand Rapids: Eerdmans, 1995), 28.

3. Marcus Borg, *Jesus*, (San Francisco: Harper, 2006), 308.

4. Karen Armstrong, *The Spiral Staircase*, (New York: Knopf, 2004), 236.

5. Tobias S. Haller, B.S.G., *Let the Reader Understand*, (The Episcopal Diocese of New York, January, 2002), 19.

6. Barbara C. Crafton, E-mail sent 8/14/03.

7. The Bryan Green Society, *Bryan Green, Parson-Evangelist*, (England, 1994), 109-110.

8. Carlton Pearson, *The Gospel of Inclusion*, (Azusa Press, 2006.)

9. *The Book of Common Prayer*, (New York: The Church Hymnal Corp., 1979), 362.

10. Katherine Jefferts Schori, "*Evangelistic Listening*," (*Episcopal Life*), January, 2007.

11. Thomas Merton, *Seeds of Contemplation*, (New York: New Directions, 1949), 21.

Afterword

1. T. S. Eliot: *The Complete Poems and Plays, Four Quartets,* "Little Gidding," (New York: Harcourt Brace Jovanovich, 1971), 145.

978-0-595-48004-3
0-595-48004-7

Printed in the United States
202617BV00004B/208-306/P